gangbusters: strategies for prevention and intervention

Lonnie Jackson

American Correctional Association Staff

Reginald A. Wilkinson, President

James A. Gondles, Jr. , Executive Director

Gabriella M. Daley, Director, Communications and Publications

Leslie A. Maxam, Assistant Director, Communications and Publications

Alice Fins, Publications Managing Editor

Michael Kelly, Associate Editor

Sherry Wulfekuhle, Editorial Assistant

Dana M. Murray, Graphics and Production Manager

Michael Selby, Graphics and Production Associate

Cover design by Michael Selby. Cover image provided by © 1994 PhotoDisc, Inc.

Printed in the United States of America by Graphic Communications, Inc., Upper Marlboro, MD.

ISBN 1-56991-082-0

This publication may be ordered from:
American Correctional Association
4380 Forbes Boulevard
Lanham, Maryland 20706-4322
1-800-222-5646

For information on publications and videos available from ACA, contact our World Wide Web home page at: http://www.corrections.com/aca

Library of Congress Cataloging-in-Publication Data

Jackson, Lonnie
  Gangbusters : strategies for prevention and intervention / by Lonnie Jackson.
    p. cm.
  ISBN 1-56991-082-0 (pbk.)
    1. Gangs—United States. 2. Gang members—United States—Rehabilitation. 3. Gang members—United States—Rehabilitation—Case studies. 4. Problem youth—Behavior modification—United States—Case studies. I. Title
HV6439.U5J33 1998
364.1'06'60973—dc21

                      98-20673
                       CIP

This book is dedicated to
my beautiful mother, Anna Mary, who continues to be
the driving influence in my life, and to Devonte, my wonderful son.

table of contents

Introduction
    James A. Gondles, Jr. ix

Acknowledgments xi

Preface xiii

Section One:
    Understanding Gang Mentality: The Beginning
    of a Gang Intervention Program

Chapter 1
    The Case for Gang Intervention Programs
    in Correctional Institutions. 1

Chapter 2
    Why Youths Are Attracted to and Join Gangs 11

Chapter 3
    The Mind-set of Gang Members: Understanding
    Gang Mentality 25

Chapter 4
    Understanding Gang Dynamics and Culture; How
    Gangs Communicate and Intimidate: Gang Graffiti,
    Handsigns, and Vernacular. 39

Section Two:
    Breaking Through Gang Mentality: Getting a Gang
    Intervention Program Underway

Chapter 5
    The Committed Facilitator: The Cornerstone of Any
    Successful Gang-intervention Program 45

Chapter 6
    Intervention Strategies to Help Gang-involved Youths
    See the Need to Turn Their Lives Around. 49

Chapter 7
    Need for Enhanced Programs 87

Chapter 8
    Beyond the Walls: The Critical Need for
    Aftercare Programs 99

Chapter 9
    Examining Rap Music 117

Section Three:
    Starting a New Program

Chapter 10
    Questions and Answers for Administrators: Why Give
    Ourselves More Headaches? 127

Chapter 11
    Blueprint for a Successful Gang-suppression Program
    In Detention and Correctional Institutions 137

Chapter 12
    Finding Support for Your Project 145

Chapter 13
    Evaluating Your Program 149

Chapter 14
    Other Minorities in Gangs 151

References 155

Appendices

Appendix A
  Oregon Youth Authority 159

Appendix B
  Testimonials 161

Appendix C
  Glossary 165

introduction

This book is intended not only for those working in the criminal justice system, but for everyone who has been or may be affected by the problems our disenfranchised and troubled youth face today. It is intended as an aid to anyone attempting to have an impact on the root causes of youth violence, crime, and the aimlessness afflicting many of America's young people. Making no pretense to offering solutions to every aspect of this national problem, this book shows there is much that can be done to improve the prospect of having an impact on or even reversing the trends of gang violence that have plagued so many communities.

During ACA's 127th Congress of Corrections in Orlando, Florida, in 1997, the Delegate Assembly passed the Public Correctional Policy on At-Risk Children, Youth, and Families. Lonnie Jackson's book goes a long way toward fulfilling the goals of various aspects of this policy, including: "Educate fellow correctional practitioners, others in the criminal justice system, at-risk children and families, educators, clergy, business leaders, medical professionals, legal professionals, etc., as to what are the characteristics of at-risk children and families, what can be done to lessen the risk, what services are available and where they can receive them."

Jackson describes how his program accomplishes some of the major objectives of this policy, such as "Encourage and support long-term commitments to a range of initiatives that include: a balanced range of community-based services available and accessible for high risk and delinquent youth." Indeed, not only does the program have partnerships within the community to provide services and jobs for its youth, it also requires former members of violent gangs to preach nonviolence to younger children thus fulfilling another part of the policy: "Anti-violence programs [should be] available to families and to all children at an early age in the schools and the community." Jackson also uses "early intervention programs such as parent education and skills development, family preservation and support services," to help youth become contributing members of society.

ACA is proud to publish this work. It offers some concrete steps that others may use to turn around gang-involved youth. We hope our readers feel inspired to emulate such a program and positively intervene in the lives of this vulnerable segment of the youth population. For more information on gangs and delinquency programs, contact the American Correctional Association at 1-800-ACA-JOIN.

James A. Gondles, Jr.
Executive Director
American Correctional Association

acknowledgments

I first want to thank and give praise to God who is my highest power. There are many, many people I would like to acknowledge. While I cofounded and coordinated the programs described in this book, I had tremendous help and support every step of the way from concerned, committed and insightful professionals. Without their knowledge and support, none of these programs could have materialized.

The MacLaren Youth Correctional Facility's superintendents all have been instrumental in the development and implementation of these programs. Without Superintendent William Carey's full support, the Minority Youth Concerns Program would not have gotten off the ground. His successors, as superintendents of MacLaren, gave us their full support as well. Rick Hill, currently the director of the Oregon Youth Authority, and Robert Jester, Area Coordinator for the Oregon Youth Authority's Northern Valley Region, have been unwavering in their support of our Minority Youth Concerns Program. I personally appreciate their encouragement and trust in me these past ten years and with their help we have been able to accomplish things that have exceeded our expectations. Their dedication and leadership to our vision have been invaluable. Current MacLaren Superintendent Gary Lawhead continues that tradition of support.

We also had the support of many staff members, including Karen Brazeau, Deputy Director of the Oregon Youth Authority; Roger Wilder, who cofounded the Minority Youth Concerns Program; Roxie Lee, Linda and Rick Hamilton, Vastie Witherspoon, Cathie Martin, Chanissa Weaver, Sam Pierce, Brian Florip, Tim

French, Marlin Hutton, Jim Nanson, Sam White, Curt Fiesel, Derrick Ingram, Robyn Cole, Marva Fabien, Tanya Snyder, Joan Dalton, John Pendergrass, David Molstad, Catarino Cavazos, and others who volunteered numerous hours helping us to get the program up and running.

The African American Male Transition Project also required tremendous support. I acknowledge the contributions of Thomas Hardy, Ron Weaver, Phil Cox, Damon Parsons, Rachael Gonzalez, Robert Richardson, Marcus Branch, Stephanie Pittman, Harold Williams, Barbara King, and David Jones.

I appreciate the help Nancy Hill and John Rodgers gave me in the writing and editing of this book.

I want to express my deepest, heartfelt thanks to Alice Fins, publications managing editor for the American Correctional Association, for her wonderful support, patience, encouragement, enthusiasm, and, most of all, her belief in me and our book project.

My sincere appreciation for the youth courageous enough to take part in our program. Without their willingness to take the deepest possible look into themselves and their lives, this program could not have happened. The young men who have examined their lives, their motivations, their biases, and their assumptions, admitted the need to change and then had the perseverance to turn their lives around have my unwavering respect and admiration.

I would like to thank my brothers Donnell and Jeffrey for their ongoing support, and Sharon Woods, my incredible mother-in-law. Finally, I would like to thank my mother for her sacrifices, her belief in me, her determination, her gentleness, and her never-ending support and encouragement.

And thank you to my young son who gives me a reason to keep smiling no matter what the day brings. He is truly a blessing from God.

—Lonnie Jackson

preface

African-American males in the United States have been killing each other at alarming rates for years. Homicide will claim the lives of more young black males in the United States this year than diseases, automobile accidents, plane crashes, natural calamities, or any other cause. Unlike some of their ancestors who were killed at the hands of their slave masters, lynched by mobs, or killed in wars, their lives will not be taken in a struggle for freedom or world peace.

Instead, they will be murdered by other Americans whose residence might be within a few hundred yards of their own and whose family circumstances are remarkably similar to theirs. This phenomenon has reached epidemic proportions with the recent explosion of gangs. Originally organized largely for the purpose of selling crack cocaine, these gangs have become a substitute family for many youths looking for security, a sense of belonging, and protection in unsafe neighborhoods.

The Portland Police Bureau's pamphlet *Gangs/Pandillas* defines gangs as "a group of people who interact among themselves to the exclusion of other groups, have a group name, claim a neighborhood or territory and engage in criminal or antisocial behavior on a regular basis." Gang members commit violent crimes at a rate three times that of nongang delinquents. And gang-involved youths are more frequently victimized by violent crime than the rest of the general population.

A 1989 survey of law enforcement officials determined that there were 1,500 gangs in forty-five American cities, with 87 percent of the identifiable gang population made up of African Americans or Hispanics. According to the National Institute of Justice, law enforcement agencies in the United States are confronted with the presence of more than 23,388 gangs and 664,906 gang members (Office of Juvenile Justice and Delinquency Prevention, 1995). Updated surveys would show that gangs and youth violence, once perceived as inner-city afflictions involving mainly ethnic minorities, have become frighteningly pervasive problems in suburbs and rural towns as well, and appear to be expanding in quantity and intensity. More and more youths infatuated with African-American and Hispanic gang lifestyles are emulating or joining gangs. Gang members cut across ethnic, economic, and rural/urban boundaries.

A recent study, conducted at the University of Chicago, estimated that 300 American cities with populations of 10,000 or more are experiencing problems with youth gangs (Spergel, 1991). It is fair to say that as we approach the late 1990s, there is not a community in this country that is not concerned about the actual or potential threats to their physical safety and emotional well-being posed by the violent and antisocial conduct of individual youths and youth gangs.

In this book, Lonnie Jackson, the director of one of the country's most effective gang intervention programs, offers insight into reasons youths are attracted to gangs and ways to prevent, confront, and reverse gang mentality. Jackson details how he and his coworkers at Oregon's MacLaren Youth Correctional Facility have successfully intervened in gangs in the juvenile correction system and directed hard-core gang members away from the lure of the gang lifestyle.

Jackson first encountered gangs as a child in his gang-infested neighborhood in South Central Los Angeles. As he grew up in the "hood," he made many of the same assumptions about life and his future that gang members often make.

Fortunately, Jackson's mother was determined that he would make something of his life. Without telling her son, she filled out and submitted an application to Willamette University in Oregon. "I didn't really care about getting a good education," Jackson admits. "But I was interested in playing sports, so when I was accepted, I agreed to go."

Once there, Jackson confronted his own biases and gained insight into the social problems from which gangs stem. "Attending Willamette was one of the most important events in my life.

Willamette was a well-respected private school with high academic standards. I knew blacks were in the minority in our country, but I had grown up in a black neighborhood and went to schools that were predominantly black. I had the culture shock of my life when I got to Willamette. I was overwhelmed by the whiteness of it. I felt like an alien in the way I dressed, in my attitudes, in my background. I was definitely out of my comfort zone and covered up by being 'hard,' acting like a tough guy and assuming a macho attitude. I made sure I created an unapproachable image with my clothes, my hat, and the shades (sunglasses) I wore.

"I had no idea what to do in college. I was totally unprepared. I didn't know how to select courses. I didn't know how to be a good student. I didn't have books, or a notebook, or a backpack. I didn't know how to take notes or how to study. I didn't care. I just wanted to get through the first year and get back home to be with my friends.

"I associated with some black students, but we came from different backgrounds. I grew up in an inner-city, and most of the other African-American students did not know that life at all. I wanted to go home to hang out with the fellas and to have a good time. To 'kick it,' as we would say.

"I didn't eat in the cafeteria because as one the few black students, I felt isolated and alone. I was put on academic probation after the first semester. I was on the verge of failing. But then I had the good fortune to have some mentors. Two people in particular, Professor Bothun and Jackie Louville, saw some potential in me and came to bat for me with the academic affairs committee. They got me to consider what I'd lose if I left.

"By the end of the first year, I started looking in the mirror and thinking about what my friends would think of me when I went back home. I knew they'd accept me. But I knew I'd changed. I thought about what they would be doing. I knew they'd still be hanging out. They hadn't had the opportunity I had. I knew people in Willamette would not necessarily care if I left, but I also realized I would not ever have this chance again to make something of myself.

"I changed my attitude and started accepting people. This was the hardest thing I had ever done. It didn't happen overnight, but Willamette was not going to change for me. I was the one who had to make adjustments if I was going to be successful.

"Little by little, I did a better job academically and people started responding to me differently. My grades improved. I projected a more positive image. By the time I graduated after four years, I was involved in campus activities and Willamette had become home to me.

"Part of what kept me persevering was my mother's continued support. She was so proud to have a son in college. I did not want to disappoint her. She was the most influential person in my life and if it had not been for her belief in me and her unconditional support, I would not have made it.

"I came to realize that a lot of young men of color go to college and fail because people of color who come from backgrounds similar to mine do not always understand the importance of education. We have not been taught to set goals. People often give up when they are out of their comfort zone—when they are unprepared, overwhelmed, and experience such a drastic culture shock. I didn't even know what a major was or what it took to graduate when I first arrived at college. It is no wonder I thought that the easiest thing to do was to give up and go home."

After graduating with a degree in sociology, Jackson accepted a job as a counselor at MacLaren Youth Correctional Facility, the largest juvenile detention facility in Oregon. He worked daily with minority youths incarcerated for serious crimes. Realizing that minority students had treatment issues unique to their culture, he cofounded the Minority Youth Concerns Program with coworker Roger Wilder.

"I saw similarities between the youths I was working with and who I had been when I first entered Willamette. Like me, the boys in the MacLaren Youth Correctional Facility were not thinking about tomorrow. They were hanging with the fellas, trying to impress girls. They wanted to 'kick it,' take it easy, and were not motivated to do something with their lives. I knew I could have ended up incarcerated, too, if I had not had the support of my mother and the support of my mentors and others at Willamette University. I believed that if these kids got the right kind of support, they, too, could turn their lives around."

Jackson has worked on a daily basis with youths of diverse ethnic and social backgrounds who have been incarcerated for serious crimes. He now heads the Minority Services Office statewide for the Oregon Youth Authority (See Appendix A for a description), a state agency created to oversee and administer juvenile corrections statewide. He has been instrumental in making significant changes in the way gang-affected and gang-involved youth are perceived and treated throughout the state. His program has been written about in many publications, he has spoken at numerous workshops and conferences throughout the country, and he is recognized throughout the United States as a leader in gang-intervention strategies.

In this book, Jackson explores the reasons youths join gangs and the mind-sets that keep intelligent, capable young men caught in a cycle of self-destructive and criminal behavior. He provides a specific, concrete plan for an intervention program that has successfully helped gang-involved youths reclaim their lives. He talks about the need for culturally sensitive, committed staff. While the program he uses for a model addresses the specific needs of African-American youths, the principles discussed are, with minor adjustments, universally applicable. Almost all of them have proven effective for intervention or suppression on both sides of correctional facility walls.

Kathryn Martin, MSW
Portland Social and Family Services
Portland, Oregon

Section I

understanding gang mentality: the beginning of a gang intervention program

1

the case for gang intervention programs in correctional institutions

The Birth of the Minority Youth Concerns Program at MacLaren Youth Correctional Facility

The author spent the first eighteen years of his life in the heart of gang territory in South Central Los Angeles, California before moving to Salem, Oregon to attend Willamette University. Gangs were a way of life in his neighborhood, and his mother wanted him as far away from the temptations of gangs as she could send him. Initially, he was not thrilled with the college he attended. He felt the student population was sheltered, pampered, and did not know much about life. Fortunately, he had people who took him aside and showed him that he was the one with the bad attitude, that his potential would be lost if he continued his negative approach to life.

He took their words to heart and examined his assumptions about the world, himself, and his classmates. He applied himself to his classes, changed the way he responded to others, and graduated with a degree in sociology, committed to working on problems plaguing our country.

Full of idealism and the belief in the possibility of change, he landed a job as a counselor at the MacLaren Youth Correctional Facility. Located in Woodburn, Oregon, a small town south of Portland, the MacLaren Youth Correctional Facility campus is situated on several acres of flat, fertile soil. Aside from the fences around the one secured unit on campus, no structures barricade the property. The campus is divided into eight cottages. Each cottage is secured, and when the young men move from one area of the campus to the other, they are escorted by staff.

The long road leading to the administration building is lined with trees, and the grounds are landscaped and maintained by "students," as MacLaren Youth Correctional Facility's inhabitants are called. There are flowerbeds and trees throughout the campus.

This rather pastoral setting houses approximately 400 youths at any given time. Sentences vary from a few months to life (some complete their sentences in adult corrections), and crimes range from theft to sex offenses to murder. At the MacLaren Youth Correctional Facility, young men confined within its walls receive treatment for many problems: drug and alcohol abuse, sex issues, anger, grief, and/or violence. Students receive both individual and group counseling. They also attend classes during their incarceration, working toward a high school diploma or a General Equivalency Degree (G.E.D.)

MacLaren Youth Correctional Facility's commitment to address the complex circumstances that led to criminal behavior were consistent with this author's approach to treatment, and he began his job full of optimism and hope. However, he soon was disquieted by the overrepresentation of minority youth in this facility. Long before Los Angeles brought the gang phenomenon to the fertile, untapped regions of Oregon, there had been a troubling demographic pattern in the MacLaren Youth Correctional Facility's population.

Although African Americans and other minorities comprised only a small percentage of the state's population (approximately 1.6 percent), they were overrepresented in the correctional facility, making up 15 percent of the young men detained at the the MacLaren Youth Correctional Facility and 10.9 percent of the Oregon Youth Authority's Secure Custody (1996). The African-American population was similarly disproportionate at the Oregon State Penitentiary.

Equally troubling was the consistently high recidivism rate among African-American juvenile offenders. Many of them had served time at the MacLaren Youth Correctional Facility, conformed

2

their behavior to staff expectations, and were released, only to reoffend — usually for a more serious crime than the one for which they previously had been incarcerated.

We had to admit that we were not making a significant differ-ence in the lives of the young African-American men we encoun-tered during the months, and sometimes years, we had them. Some clear and distinct patterns were emerging. When they came to the institution, the smart young men would "front" the program, com-plying with our behavior codes and rules to earn a quick return to the community.

At the other extreme, we had youths who were constant behav-ioral problems. They frequently were locked down because they maintained a hard-core gang image. When these students got together, whether at the school, in the recreation areas, or other places they could congregate, they continued to perpetuate the gang and street-life mentality. Frequently, they would say things like, "When I get out, I'm gonna kick it with the homies," or, "I'm gonna get out and bust on a crab (or bust on a slob)," meaning they intended to get into a fight with their rival gang members (See Appendix C for definitions of slang terms). Many made state-ments about "getting my slang on," which referred to selling drugs. They talked about "getting this hooptie," an old car. Clearly, their conversations were not about returning to the community to be productive. Instead, they talked about continuing their delinquent, negative, gang lifestyle, and posing a danger to their community.

We concluded that mere detention, combined with the generally accepted approaches for handling juvenile delinquents in correc-tional facilities, were not enough to bring about significant changes in the attitudes and motivations of most of the African-American youths incarcerated at the MacLaren Youth Correctional Facility.

For many reasons, the conventional approaches we had been using were ineffective. Many of our youths found life within the confines of the facility to be no worse than the lives they had been living on the outside. They ate three square meals a day, the adults posed no threat to their safety, and they had little to fear from the youths around them because of the constant security mea-sures in effect.

They had fewer decisions to make than they had before they were incarcerated. Less was required of them to make it to the next day. Essentially, all they had to do was wake up, eat, attend classes and group discussions, and sleep. While the MacLaren

Youth Correctional Facility has a history of innovative treatment programs, many gang-affected youths found the programs irrelevant to their lives and only went through the motions of participating. They did little to grow or learn. They did not have to prove anything except that they could pass a specified period of time without seriously misbehaving. With these as their only challenges and with average sentence times of three months to three years, one hardly could expect them to emerge as responsible citizens, motivated and ready for gainful employment, who were willing to be positive influences on their families and communities.

For many years, the MacLaren Youth Correctional Facility has had a number of good and generally effective treatment programs for sex offenders, violent offenders, youths with drug and alcohol abuse issues, and boys with anger-management problems. Although these programs have merit, they were not geared to help urban youth with a real hard-core, street-life gang mentality. Existing programs failed to pierce the particular mind-set such youths were bringing to our facility in increasing numbers.

To get to the root of the problem, we needed a program that addressed the issues of minority recidivism as a treatment issue. This included identifying factors unique to the experience of most minority youth — factors that were causing criminal behavior. We needed to address these issues in a way that would reduce the likelihood of a young man's return to criminal behavior after incarceration.

Such a program, we knew, would have to do more than instruct. It would have to convey an authentic understanding of how the youths came to be the way they were and to instill in them a sincere concern about their own futures.

The MacLaren Youth Correctional Facility's administration was aware of the problem and issues with gang-affiliated youth. When we presented our concerns and ideas to the MacLaren Youth Correctional Facility Superintendent William Carey and his administrative staff, we received an immediate affirmative response to our proposal to start a program that would address the specific needs of gang-affiliated youths. Even though Carey only had been at the MacLaren Youth Correctional Facility for a few years, he took a stand and allowed us to undertake a very controversial program. There were already a number of treatment programs on campus, and he was courageous to support one dealing specifically with gangs.

Some staff and others involved in the MacLaren Youth Correctional Facility's programs were worried that a program specifically for minorities would cause serious problems. They feared minorities might band together and plan escapes. They feared that African Americans and Hispanics would become more militant, that gangs would become more powerful and better organized. They feared assaults on staff and attacks on other students. They were concerned that gangs would recruit new members and that there would be conflicts between rival gangs.

Our program had strong administrative support, which is crucial for any program, especially a new one, and such support is especially critical for a controversial program. Carey was well aware of the concerns of staff, but he gave us his full support. Without his belief in what we wanted to do, the program never may have happened. His successors gave us their full support, as well. We also had the support of many staff members and others who volunteered numerous hours helping us get the program up and running.

Because of this type of support, we were able to design a program to meet our objectives. On October 14, 1987, the Minority Youth Concerns Program was instituted at the MacLaren Youth Correctional Facility. Lonnie Jackson, this author, was its first director.

Our Greatest Challenge: "Show me a reason not to bang."

After talking with youth-serving professionals throughout the United States about their experiences with minority populations, particularly with gang members, the author learned that their situations have been similar to those the staff experienced before the gang-intervention program. A gang-involved youth in a state correctional facility may give every outward indication of being reformed by incarceration. However, such indication may be nothing more than fool's gold dropped into the pans of the authorities by an intelligent, manipulative person, cleverly concealing his actual intention to get back to the streets and return to the criminal lifestyle.

The author met a Hispanic male during a visit to another state. He was introduced as one of the best behaved, hardest working students in the facility. He had attained the highest level possible in the institution. But his clothes and the way he projected himself showed that he was still promoting his gang image.

When the author met with him one-on-one, he praised him for doing well and asked what his plans were once he returned to the community. He said he would return to banging when he got out. The author asked him why he would do that after doing so well in the institution, with people speaking so highly of him. He looked directly at him and said, "Because nobody has shown me a reason not to bang."

His response, with all its simplicity and frankness, expresses our challenge in a nutshell. Too few of our juvenile correctional facilities in this country are giving young men reasons not to return to gang activity when they are released. Sadly, some institutions even have gang behavior within their walls.

If juvenile corrections professionals fail to make the effort to understand the thought patterns, values, and attitudes of gang-involved youths and fail to offer programs designed to change attitudes and ways of thinking, we are doing an injustice to the youth and the communities into which they are released. We all should aspire to Dr. Martin Luther King, Jr.'s dream in which his children "will not be judged by the color of their skin, but by the content of their character." Nevertheless, we must take notice of the common experiences and factors that, for decades, have kept conventional treatment plans from having their intended corrective impact on certain ethnic populations, particularly African Americans and Hispanics.

We have a growing number of minority youth who require a comprehensive strategy of treatment and intervention. These young men must contend with multiple issues. Like the sex offender, the addict, or the alcoholic in denial, these young men are intensely resistant to reform. Their gangs and their gang lifestyles are their loves. They are willing to die for their "sets."

You cannot overcome their passionate devotion to their gang lifestyle with minimal or token effort. The challenge requires a comprehensive approach that makes them check their thinking, their value system, their actions, and their way of living. The gang mentality must be seen as a treatment issue and addressed in an extensive, systematic, and personal manner by a culturally sensitive, well-trained staff.

We have a golden opportunity to work with these young men when they come to our facilities for a set period of time. We may have some for six months, others for a year, or more. Regardless of the length of time they are incarcerated, they are in a structured environment. We know where they are. Their minds are not clouded by drugs and alcohol. We can expose them to information and education to show them alternatives to gangs. We can deal with the mind-set that makes gang activities not only acceptable, but appealing as well.

There is a culture emerging that is part of today's gang phenomenon, including handsigns, language, graffiti, tattoos, and dress. The norms of such cultures account for a number of actions and decisions many of us find alien — tattoos, a willingness to endure a "beatdown" or to shoot up a house full of people, loyalty to one's "homies," and depersonalized views of other people based on their gender or the color of their clothing.

We have to do more than object to or put-down gangs when we work with gang-involved youths. We must offer these young men hope. We must remind them of their connection to a more noble and valuable culture.

There are certain motivations and needs that seem to be universal. However, we can better meet the treatment needs of the youths we serve when we demonstrate an awareness of and sensitivity to their cultural backgrounds. Cultural sensitivity increases the youth's receptivity to the information we want to share with them. It also helps the youths see their connection to a greater cultural history instead of how they currently live through a series of isolated, insignificant chance occurrences. This cultural identity increases their feelings of self-worth and helps them see the need to change.

Additionally, these streetwise youths are more likely to reject or ignore generic, culturally void, or neutral instruction. Unless something relates directly to them, their situation, and their lives, they will not be open. They will not listen. Thus, all superintendents who know they have a significant gang population are encouraged to develop a culturally specific program to address the issues that have led youths to join gangs or to cure those who are infatuated with gangs.

Individuals working in institutions housing gang-involved youths proactively must develop and refine programs that address gang involvement as a treatment issue and tailor treatment to get through the mind-set and defenses of urbanized, hard-core, streetwise youths. Otherwise, we will have perpetual aimlessness and recidivism among the gang-affiliated population.

Every human body has the same nutritional needs. But the foods and dishes used to satisfy that need vary greatly throughout the world. Our menu of treatment approaches must be similarly diverse to restore our youths to societal and mental health.

The cultural sensitivity necessary for effective gang intervention includes, but is not necessarily limited to, race and ethnicity. Indeed, there is a culture that increasingly transcends ethnic identity alone. These young men need specific help in seeing the need to end their association with gangs. They need to be exposed to alternatives to that lifestyle. They need a staff who understands the real reasons they chose the gang lifestyle in the first place.

We cannot let obstacles or objections from staff prevent us from addressing the unique issues of gang-involved youths. We do not do that with drug or sex offenders. Yet, at many juvenile correctional facilities, there is resistance to gang-specific treatment programs.

Some staff think that because gang members are not causing problems, there is no need for an intervention program. As already indicated, it is not unusual for gang youths to go along with the program while they are locked up because they know it is in their best interest to conform. However, when they get out, they are going to go right back to gang-banging because they have not been shown a need to change.

As long as incarcerated gang members are "talking the talk" and showing no indication that they are willing to get out of gangs, there is a problem in your facility. The youth must be shown another way to live, to learn how they can be productive, and how to make something of their lives. It is not in the best interest of the community to return a gang member to the same neighborhood to continue to commit crimes.

Post-traumatic Stress Disorder and Other Psychological Concerns

We need to consider the backgrounds of many of our youths when creating a program to meet their needs. The mind-sets we encounter often are the product of a young mind trying to cope with traumas in a manner consistent with the surrounding environment. Many of the youths we receive and those in other juvenile correctional facilities have been traumatized repeatedly during their childhoods. They may have heard the sounds of gunshots and stray bullets whizzing around them at night. They may have seen their friends die, and their parents and siblings beaten and abused in the home. The treatment these young men receive at least must look for signs of post-traumatic stress disorder and deal with these conditions where they are found.

In our initial assessment of each incoming youth, we look for signs of post-traumatic stress and other psychological or mental health problems, and request full mental health evaluations if we suspect that deeper work would benefit the youth. Our goal is to help this population deal with their feelings and work through them. In doing so, we hope to free them to embrace the humane, caring person hidden inside of them in the hope that they will feel comfortable shedding the hard exterior mantle they have worn for too long.

For example, one young man in our program saw his mother arguing with her boyfriend. The boyfriend threw her into his car and drove off. She has been missing ever since. Her body has never been found. He has to deal with the fact that he had the last chance to save his mother's life but he could not do anything. Occasionally, he is suicidal. His father is a heroin addict. Had we not taken his horrifying experiences into account, we might never have found his psychological access point and begun the tedious process of reorienting him to this world. Much work lies ahead, but before we can talk meaningfully about society's expectations of him, we first must help him deal with the deeply submerged scars ripped into his psyche for more than a decade.

Our goal is empowerment. We want our youths not only to see the need to no longer associate with gang members and to stop negative behavior, but we also want them to develop confidence, self-esteem, and the social, educational, and technical foundation required to become self-sufficient, law-abiding young men.

While our program has focused on the African-American gang member, our efforts can be modified readily to address the culturally specific needs of Hispanic and Asian gang members, and young women involved in gangs and gang activities. We also would like to stress that we do not believe that staff members need to be African American to work with African-American youth (but note the cautions discussed on pages 138-140). Our staff includes whites and Hispanics, both male and female. What matters when working with gang-involved youths is not race or gender, but the individual's ability to understand the mind-set of gang members and to be able to relate to and gain the respect of the youth. One reason for this book is to help anyone interested in working with this population gain the understanding necessary to help break the mind-set that keeps our youth imprisoned in gang activities.

2

why youths are attracted to and join gangs

Background

Although some young people dress their infants in gang colors and take pictures of them with their little fingers curled and bent as if flashing gang signs, the vast majority of today's gang members were not born into their gangs. Their association with gangs was a choice they made — a choice made attractive for a number of reasons.

To put together an effective intervention or counseling strategy for these youths, we first must examine factors that make gang involvement seem a reasonable, if not attractive, way to improve their lives. In dealing with gang-affiliated youth, we have found similarities in the backgrounds of those who join gangs.

A young person may become involved in a gang for these reasons:

1. Frequent exposure to crime and violence during formative years results in desensitivity to such occurrences

2. There are few positive role models, particularly of their own ethnicity; negative influences are more common than positive ones

3. They come from unstable families, with very little parental control

4. They live in an environment lacking economic activity conducive to lawful self-sufficiency; instead, the environment breeds hopelessness and offers few reasons to believe success can be achieved through conventional means

5. Their environment lacks constructive social and recreational activities for them

6. Their social environment has a distorted set of moral values in which selfish, antisocial conduct is accepted and promoted as the acceptable norm

7. The youth believe that they have matured as far as possible; that there is not much more to look forward to except what they perceive as "low-level" jobs

8. They are entrapped into selling drugs by the lure of "living large," despite inadequate skills, education, or qualifications

9. They inhabit a culture that highly values immediate gratification, both materially and sensually

10. They suffer from low self-esteem

11. There is an absence of respected adult figures to give youths the "right word," or to affirm traditional values and standards, and to encourage the youths to keep their conduct within bounds

12. There is a natural need to ensure physical safety, to have a sense of belonging, and to form secure emotional relationships with others

13. Because they feel insignificant and powerless, youths are attracted to the power of gangs because gangs exercise considerable control over the lives of others and command the attention of public officials and the news media

A few words of caution are in order before we proceed. First, the vast majority of young African Americans and an increasing number of children of all races and socioeconomic conditions are exposed to one or more of these factors and never join gangs. So, while there is some cause and effect between these factors and gang involvement, this author is not suggesting that African-American children and their families cannot resist or overcome them.

Second, none of these factors is a justification for antisocial behavior. In fact, to encourage anyone to regard them in that light would perpetuate the problems we seek to eliminate. Having said that, let us consider how each of these factors, over time, might cause youths to regard more conventional, wholesome lifestyle choices to be unrealistic, even undesirable, for them.

Factors Leading to Gang Involvement

Factor one: Frequent exposure to crime and violence during formative years, results in desensitivity to such occurrences

Reasonable people disagree about whether violence on television and in movies causes people to commit violent acts. However, few dispute the fact that the more one is exposed to traumatic and violent events, the less unusual and less disturbing they become.

After years of having sleep interrupted by sirens and gunfire and seeing dead bodies surrounded by onlookers on the streets of his neighborhood, a child may come to regard violence as natural and unavoidable. He may come to feel violence is no big deal, especially if the adults in his home are violent towards him and each other. If he has been beaten up at home and at school, and no place is safe, why not take one more "beatdown," a common gang-initiation, in order to be somebody?

Once in the gang, he may see no reason not to hurt others. "I might as well get mine while I can. What difference does it make if I have to take somebody out to get paid? Nobody lives forever. Besides, my homies got my back."

Factor two: There are few positive role models, particularly of their own ethnicity; negative influences are more common than positive ones

When children's parents, relatives, or close family friends are enjoyably engaged in an activity, the children are more likely to want to attempt it themselves. They gain confidence that they, too, can accomplish it. These successful adults are role models for the children.

Many professionals are in the same profession as one of their parents, such as Liza Minnelli, Natalie Cole, Ken Griffey, Jr., and Barry Bonds, as well as many teachers and police officers. Many of today's gangsters do not have such role models. Most grew up without their fathers or any other permanent adult male in their home or in their lives.

Charles Barkley was right when he said in a television commercial, "I am not a role model. I am not paid to be a role model. Just because I can play basketball doesn't mean that I should raise your kids." Lost in the hoopla over the commercial was the distinction Barkley and Nike were making between sports heroes or heroes in other endeavors, and role models.

A role model is someone who a person can relate to in intimate person-to-person moments, not under the glare and spotlight of publicity. The modeling must be authentic to be effective. Well-known self-improvement lecturer and author Anthony Robbins encourages the frequent practice of "modeling" to anyone who wants to maximize their potential and experience success in personal and professional endeavors.

Before anyone can be successful, or even begin to pursue a goal, he or she must believe that the goal can be attained. Young people are most likely to chose a model who looks like them, sounds like them, and appears to be facing the same obstacles and injustices as they are encountering.

We understand that many, if not most, of the youths we encounter do not know many people who have attained success through conventional or lawful means. More often, they see financial and professional success as something conservative white people control and deny to African-American people and others, like themselves.

With no one to serve as proof of their own potential, they readily respond to people who look and sound like them and appear to face the same obstacles and injustices in life. Many of these people reinforce the negative messages the youths have heard throughout their formative years about societal and other barriers to having a good life. Believing that the menu of their life's options is very short, they choose a direction that they believe will improve their condition.

Factor three: They come from unstable families, with little parental control

Most of the youth we see do not regard their parent, who most often is a single mother, as a role model. In fact, the parent(s) generally have no ability to influence the actions or decisions of their children. After repeated failure, many parents stop trying to help their children lead productive lives.

We do not want to place unfair blame on parents. Often, these youths are raised in single-family homes with the mother as the sole provider. She often faces serious economic problems. She may not be well educated herself, and it is likely that her salary does not meet her family's financial needs. She may hold more than one job. She may not have the time she needs or wishes she had to take care of her kids. She may go to work before her children are up and not return home until after the school day has ended. She may be on welfare, and her checks may be inadequate to meet her family's needs. When she tries to find a job, she may discover that she makes less, not more, after taxes are taken out of her paycheck than she has made on welfare.

She also may have other personal issues. She probably does not have the financial resources to get her children tutoring if they need extra help in school. She might not be able to afford the fees to get her children into sports and, even if she can, she may not have transportation to get them to and from practices and games. Because they are exposed to television, her children may want things she cannot afford; so, they may become angry or find illegal ways to get what they want. Besides, the parent may have been a teenager when her children were born and never may have had positive role models to show her what good parenting involves. Then, after working hard all week, the mother may feel that she deserves weekends off and may visit friends, and leave the children unsupervised.

By the time our youths were big enough and bold enough to lie, conceal, and even physically strike back at their parents, these youths have exercised more overt control over their parents' households than their parents have. After losing one power struggle after another to their children and realizing the children do not want help or guidance, the parents simply may concede defeat to hold on to what is left of their sanity. Perhaps more tragic is the family in which the parents are clueless because their child has honed the skills of distracting, manipulating, and lying. These are some of the conditions that exist in many young gang-affected youth's homes.

Factor four: They live in an environment lacking economic activity conducive to lawful self-sufficiency; instead, the environment breeds hopelessness and offers few reasons to believe that success can be achieved through conventional means

While there are exceptions to any rule, the overwhelming majority of young gangsters come from economically depressed communities. Economic depression is nothing new to many African-American communities. Yet, as mentioned earlier, neither this, nor any other factor discussed in this chapter, should be considered a justification for gang involvement and criminal activities.

These factors, however, are influential in steering youth toward gangs. Building on previous discussions, one would hardly expect to find many positive role models where there is little day-to-day success. There are many good people in such communities, many of whom have been concerned about improving the lot of each generation long before the gang phenomenon arose. Yet, economic stagnation provides no fuel for optimism.

Factor five: Their environment lacks constructive social and recreational activities for youths

For reasons already discussed, many of today's youths must look outside the family for role models and emotional support. Yet, in the environments we have described, there is a considerable lack of social and recreational activities for the youths. Again, this is not to say there are not some in every community, but clearly there are not enough to deal with the population. And many of the well-intended, youth-focused programs simply do not appeal to youths at risk for gang involvement.

Communities without a strong enough economic base to construct their own facilities for recreational and social activities must depend on municipal and county governments or an external benefactor to provide the facilities. This does little to create a feeling of community empowerment. However, it is better to have them, from whatever the source, than not to have them at all. There simply are not enough of them to meet the expanding population of youths in need of positive direction. With increasing pressure on all levels of government to stop growing and to cut taxes, we can expect less, not more, assistance from all levels of the government. However much they might want to help, financial restraints may prevent it.

Factor six: Their social environment has a distorted set of moral values in which selfish, antisocial conduct is accepted and promoted as the accepted norm

Rational, pragmatic thinking is not valued among many youth today. Where their parents would consider it a negative statement about someone to say he or she is "screwed up," some gangsters use the Spanish word for crazy, *loco*, and proudly refer to themselves as "loced out," perhaps realizing that one must be a bit insane to voluntarily enter a world of "beatdowns," where they face the possibility of being a victim of a drive-by shooting.

For the sake of being part of something larger than themselves, they subscribe to a code of conduct which says that the worst thing you can be is "soft," or a "punk." They are indoctrinated to believe that the only people to care about are one's "home-boys," the members of their gang "set." They must not drop the exterior mantle of being hard, even when affirming their extraordinary allegiance to each other. They must look tough, intimidating, and angry, except when getting high on drugs or forty-ounce bottles of malt liquor in the security of the "set."

Being hard means you do not walk erect like some punk businessman in a "monkey suit." You keep your shoulders slouched and your head down a bit. You wear mostly black, very baggy clothes, so nobody can give an accurate physical description of you to the police.

So pervasive is this new cultural attitude of hardness among today's youth that from a very early age, many kids, even those with no desire to get into a gang, dress, walk, and talk as if they were gang members. This imitative conduct sometimes is motivated by a desire to be thought of as a gangster. Such kids are called "wanna-bes." In other instances, such behavior is motivated by a desire to be left alone. If they look tough, they reason, maybe the bullies will pick on somebody else.

Most gangsters have no regard for marriage, and in a warped sense of manhood, reinforce in each other the notion that it is a sign of weakness for a man to become emotionally committed to one sex partner. Girls and women are trophies to be seen with and tools for the release of sexual tension, often referred to in such terms as "bustin' a nut," "gettin' G'd," "knockin' the boots," or "gettin' waxed."

A youth who talks to such fellows about making a commitment, planning a family, or supporting his children and their mother is likely to lose standing with them. "Sex? Everybody's gonna do it. Just do not get involved emotionally — sprung on the girl — and go soft. Hell, if she gets pregnant, that's her problem."

Unfortunately, it is true that people from all walks of life would prefer to have sensual pleasure without responsibility. A child who sees his peers jumping off the springboard into the deep end of a pool all summer, experiencing nothing but pleasure, probably will decide that he at least wants to give it a try. And, in too many cases, there is no one to help him consider other options.

Factor seven: The youth believe they have matured as far as possible; that there is not much more to look forward to except what they perceive as "low-level" jobs

Despite the fact that many gangsters could not find gainful employment, live independently, and be self-sufficient, they often have high absentee rates and act out at school. They eventually drop out, reasoning that school is for punks anyway. They do not need to be in school. They are men, ready to "live large." An expression commonly heard among today's youths is, "I'm getting paid," which means they are making money.

They sometimes will say that they want a job, and despite the fact that they lack the skills to qualify for most minimum-wage jobs, they will say, "I ain't goin' for no burger-flippin' job at Mickie D's."

This attitude is the product of a misapplication of self-respect. The reasoning is that, "I deserve to have what I want in life. I do not need any more education. I do not need training. I'm a man. I need money." This attitude would get a person laughed out of a job interview with any organization in today's society except one — a gang.

Factor eight: They are entrapped into selling drugs by the lure of "living large," despite inadequate skills, education, or qualifications

Gangs welcome people who see no need to continue the pursuit of self-development. Once initiated, gangsters gain a sense of being somebody important in their world, someone able to handle serious responsibilities. The job description might read like this:

"Watch the backs of your homeboys against attacks from sucker crews in rival gangs. We got to do an occasional jack-back or some other kind of dirt, but it's only to enforce our control of our turf, you know, the geographic area we be claimin'. Forget them sucka jobs! Sell a little crack from time to time to wacked out suckas and you be handling thousands every month!

"There is no clock to punch, but you gots to be ready at all times. Be there. Be down. You'll get to ride in Caddies, Benzo's, Beamers, Jeeps, you name it. They won't be yours, but that do not matter. You can have your hair in Geri Curls all the time if you want to. You be havin' all the hos you can handle. You be livin' large. Gold chains around your neck. Lots of money. You be clockin' them dolla's and kickin' it and loungin'! Here. Take this nine (millimeter gun). You can have it. You're down with us."

Cars, sex, money, protection, status. This is not a bad promise to a boy who has nothing.

Factor nine: They inhabit a culture that highly values immediate gratification, both materially and sensually

By now, the details of every snowflake on this snowball rolling toward gang involvement should be quite clear. The foregoing factors all build on each other for a cumulative impact on the minds of many young men today. It seems useless to leave the ghetto to get away from them, however, because when it comes to this ninth factor, it does not matter where one is.

Turn on the television and watch any music channel, and you are likely to see music videos glamorizing pimping and making big dollars daring any sucker to "step to me." (See Chapter 9 for more on the influence of rap music.)

Materialism and immediate gratification are themes repeated in most commercials on any broadcast, particularly for those the young men are most likely to watch, such as sporting events. Throughout our society, we constantly are encouraged to go for the gold, be young, have fun, and drink. Come on the show, spin the wheel of fortune, play the state lottery, and get rich now! Just do it.

These societal pressures appeal not just to youths, but also to their parents, who, with each passing day, are reminded of how little they have after so many years of living. Neither the child nor his parents is likely to watch religious or intellectually stimulating shows. The parent figure has no desire to feel guilty or inadequate, and would rather not sit through such a program. The child, in turn, has no reason or desire to sit and listen to it when something more sensually stimulating is just a click away.

Factor ten: They suffer from low self-esteem

Few thirteen-year-olds are capable of earning a legal income to support their family. However, they are more likely to see a gun or a vial of crack cocaine as means for immediate acquisition of the things they would otherwise never have — status and "bank" (money).

Most human behavior is in direct response to how people feel about themselves. Those who feel good about themselves usually seek to do good for others. Those who have low self-esteem spend a great deal of time trying to cope with their feelings of inadequacy. Sometimes, they try to better their conditions. Other times, they try to get even with people they think unfairly acquired the things in life they themselves lack.

This is often the mind-set of the youth about to enter a gang. It seems that at every turn, society is telling him, as the Madam, Miss Brooks, said to Billie Holiday in Lady Sings the Blues, "You git on 'way from 'roun' here! 'Cause you ain't nothin'! You ain't never been nothin' and you ain't gonna be nothin!" Once internalized, such perceptions of one's own potential make fairly low lifestyles appear to be their only domain.

Factor eleven: There is an absence of respected adult figures to give youths the "right word," or to affirm traditional values and standards, and to encourage youths to keep their conduct within bounds

Not that long ago, if an African American were found skipping school or misbehaving, an adult in the community would have grabbed him by the ear, gotten in his face, given him a brief lecture, a swat on the behind, and sent him on his way. The adult then would follow up with a call or a personal visit to his parents to give them the whole story. There was a kind of trust and a sense of shared responsibility in African-American communities. The Swahili saying, "It takes an entire village to raise a child," is a popular quote that once was visible in inner-city communities.

This has changed. Because of a number of factors, including the mobility of our society, wars, high rates of incarceration and homicide, and the irresponsibility and selfishness of so many adults over the past thirty years, many children do not have grandparents, uncles, ministers, or even coaches to steer them in the right direction or to simply let children know that they noticed their misbehavior and care enough about them to confront them and tell them to "get on the good foot."

Adults should be human barometers, responsibly regulating the behavior of the youngsters in our midst. Lacking responsible, caring adults, children are left to their own devices. Without role models, resources, or peers with self-esteem and good judgment, it is easy to see how the snowball picks up size and speeds toward gang involvement.

Factor twelve: There is a natural need to ensure physical safety, to have a sense of belonging, and to form secure emotional relationships with others

In many communities, sometimes hundreds of rounds of gunfire can be heard in the middle of the night. Vandalism and intimidation are everywhere. In the face of this danger, even a "good" child might consider joining a gang to feel more secure. This is not a uniquely American phenomenon, as children in South Africa, Northern Ireland, and Lebanon could attest. Self-preservation is one of the highest instincts in nature. However, the fallacy of this decision is clear: by joining a gang, one becomes a "mark," a target for harm from rival gangs.

The youths who join gangs often come from families who do not provide them with emotional stability and security. Often, they are from single parent homes with the parent absent a great deal of time. They often live in poverty and do not do well in school. Consequently, they feel lost and alone. They have few friends, no close family ties, and no adult looking out for them. In essence, they have no sense of belonging.

Gangs offer them what their family is not providing — a sense of belonging. In a gang, they have "friends" to turn to, people who will look out for them, people who will even die for them, if need be. They have someone to spend time with, to relax with, and often, for the first time in their lives, they feel they are part of something.

Factor thirteen: Because they feel insignificant and powerless, youths are attracted to the power of gangs because gangs exercise considerable control over the lives of others and command the attention of public officials and the news media

If a youth wears an athletic Starter jacket, adults fear him, thinking he is a gangster. He gets beaten up by real gangsters or "wanna-bes" and his jacket is stolen. He calls the police. They take an hour to contact him, take the information, and leave, with no promise of a follow-up investigation. "Well," he reasons, "if you can't beat 'em, join 'em."

The youth feels that society does not care about him. Because many adults misunderstand, and even fear today's youths, many youths see themselves as part of the problem, even when they would rather not be. To the extent they feel society has given up on them, they are willing to give up on themselves. When they do, another gang holds a reception.

As a gang member, he is now somebody. He can read about himself and his "homeboys" in the paper. When there's a "drive-by," the television cameras line up and interview people about their fear of gangs in the neighborhood. He feels he is part of something important.

Finally, he is getting some attention. He is somebody now. When he shows up in his "colors," people show respect. Unless he is shown where this kind of attention will lead — incarceration or death — he will continue to enjoy the power he feels he now has.

The Need for Early Prevention

While this book was originally designed to help those working with youths who already have joined gangs, all of the factors discussed here need to be recognized and addressed when a child is first vulnerable to gangs — hence the "prevention" part of the title. Community programs, educators, and other knowledgeable people need to recognize the attraction gangs have to children who fit the criteria outlined in this chapter.

If we address these issues with children who fit the profile of someone likely to be attracted to gangs *before* they join a gang, we will make giant steps toward eliminating gangs altogether. There is a tremendous need for prevention programs. To do this, we need the cooperation of corrections, educators, families, and the community. Children considered or identified as at-risk for gang involvement need mentors, tutors, afterschool programs, and counseling. Their families, including their parents, often need counseling and help from social workers. As a community, we need to provide hope and to show our young people that success and fulfillment can be within their grasp.

As stated by an article written by Donna Bownes and Sarah Ingersoll in the Office of Juvenile Justice and Delinquency Prevention's July 1997 *Juvenile Justice Bulletin*:

> As more communities attempt to prevent youth crime by developing and implementing long-term solutions, the demand for resources, best practices, and strategies continues to grow. If this country is to reduce delinquency and resultant criminality, there must be a coordinated, substantial, and sustained public and private investment of financial and human resources in families, communities, and the systems that support and protect them.

A parent and teacher education program is very helpful in prevention programs. Specific behavior can help identify a child as interested in gangs. Once identified, prevention efforts must begin immediately. Early signs include: displaying problems with family relationships; making little academic progress; having a high truancy rate; getting in trouble with school officials and police; drawing gang symbols on self and notebook paper; dressing in gang attire and making changes in hair style; playing "gang" in the neighborhood or on the schoolgrounds; using a new vocabulary; staying out all night; and living in a neighborhood that has gangs.

Programs listed in the Office of Juvenile Justice and Delinquency Prevention's July 1997 *Juvenile Justice Bulletin* that have proven effective include those that have included some or all of the following: counseling and intervention services, programs for parents that improve parenting skills, health services that provide prenatal care and health education classes, school-based programs that target at-risk behaviors, economic development and training programs including job readiness and skill development, law enforcement-sponsored programs, and comprehensive community mobilization activities.

3

the mind-set of gang members: understanding gang mentality

Why Study Gangs?

Too many people studying the thoughts and behavior of gang members do so for the wrong reasons. Some radio and television programs do little more than exploit naive minds that mistake publicity for status and glorification. They give gang-involved youths a few moments of notoriety to acquire a higher percentage of the television-viewing audience. They exploit the public appetite for sex and violence, knowing that after five commercial breaks and a preview of the next titillating topic, the viewers will cluck their tongues, say, "Wow!" and go on with their lives.

Some politicians and self-appointed leaders use gangs to advance their careers or agendas or, at the very least, to increase their name familiarity. Often well-intended, they call community summits and have open-mike sessions where people of all ages come forward and state the obvious: African Americans should stop killing African Americans; parents need to exercise control and authority over their kids; drugs are at the heart of the problem; racism is at the heart of it all; the police do not really care; the criminal justice system is too lenient; and repeat criminals need to stay locked up. The energy generated by these exercises usually provides more heat than light and all but evaporates when the last floodlight and microphone have been packed away.

Community summits *can* be very beneficial if people involved have plans for follow-up and outcomes. It is not enough to simply talk about the problem. Groups involved in gang issues need an action plan that includes education of other community members and groups, prevention efforts, and suppression efforts. These groups should include the participation and support or representatives from schools, law enforcement, corrections, the private sector, and everyone else who has an interest in problems plaguing areas that have gangs. All of these groups have a great deal at stake, and all need to communicate their concerns and lend support to the others involved in these issues. It is a community problem, and everyone involved or affected needs to work together for a solution.

To have an impact on young people, one must first gain their confidence and respect. This cannot be done without understanding gang mentality. It is critical to take a good, candid look at how gang-involved youths think, reason, and feel.

In this chapter, we will examine the various states of mind that gang-involved youths enter as they engage in various transactions. We will look at how the mind-set these youths assume affects the thoughts and actions of their peers and rivals, setting in motion a seemingly endless cycle of destructive behavior. Finally, we will examine the essential components of gang lifestyles that make them so alluring to today's youths.

The mind-set of youths considering gang involvement

A person likely to become part of a gang often experiences academic problems and feels alienated from his family and society. The youth is between the age of twelve and twenty-two and can come from any income level. Sometimes, gang involvement is generational, and the youth may have siblings who also are involved in gangs.

Gang-involved youths believe they derive four primary benefits from their gang involvement, as follows:

Identity or recognition. Being part of a gang allows a youth to achieve a level of status not possible outside the gang culture.

Protection. Many members join a gang because they live in a gang area and are subject to violence by rival gangs. Joining guarantees support in case of attack and retaliation.

Brotherhood. To the majority of gang members, the gang functions as an extension of — even a substitute for — the family. It may provide companionship lacking in the gang members' home. Older brothers and relatives may belong to the gang.

Avoiding Further Intimidation. Some members are forced to join by their peer group. Intimidation techniques range from lunch money extortion to physical beatings.

We interviewed five different young men with extensive gang and criminal histories to demonstrate gang mentality. We asked each of them the same questions. Their answers reveal similarities and patterns that provide direction for creating strategies to divert youths from gangs. Names and other identifying information have been changed or eliminated to preserve their anonymity. Otherwise, the interviews are presented intact.

MARK, 17

(Adjudicated for attempted murder)

What was your mind-set when you were gang-banging?
I didn't want to feel like a punk. If somebody rode up and tried to clown or say something about my set, I'd be like — I'd want to shoot 'em or get up with them or hurt them.

What was the mind-set of your home boys when you were gang banging?
Basically, just like me. We were all together. Whoever clown, or whoever step off on the wrong turf where they do not supposed to be at we'd be fightin' them or shoot them.

How did being in a gang make you feel?
Crazy! Crazy and, you know, wanna hurt people.

Why's that?
'Cause of the color you were wearin'. You know somebody out there gonna want to get you for wearin' the wrong color in the wrong neighborhood.

So, it made you feel crazy being in a gang?
Yeah.

Did it make you feel powerful?
Yeah. That too, 'cause I got my friends with me, too.

How did you feel about violence and weapons when you were banging?
I didn't care. I had a gun. I didn't worry 'bout nothin'.

Were you afraid to use it?
Nope.

How did you feel about gang-banging in relation to your family? Did you think about what could happen to them with you gang-banging?
I didn't let my mom know about it but she found out. I didn't try to keep it a secret.

Did you think about what could happen to them with you gang-banging?
Nope. I was just worried about myself and worried about my friends.

How did you feel about girls when you were gang-banging?
Really nothin'. They didn't do what I tell 'em, I forget 'em or somethin'.

What was your typical day like when you were gang-banging?
Everyday, you know, do not go to school. Go to my friend's house, smoke weed, sit around, go outside, listen to the radio. Watch people walk by. If they were in a rival gang or we do not like 'em, we'd start talkin' shit to them, then start fightin', whatever.

How did you feel about school?
I didn't care about school, you know? There wasn't no fun there. It be all boring and stuff, so I'd just forget it.

How did you feel about drugs? Did you sell any? What was your drug of choice?
I liked being high and drunk. I sold some. My drugs of choice were weed and alcohol.

Who were your role models? Why did you consider them such?
The older people in my set. The O.G.s (older gangsters) because
they had been through all this and they were teaching us, and
tellin' us, "you can't be punkin', you know."

CHARLES, 17

(Adjudicated for two counts of attempted murder)

What was your mind-set when you were gang banging?
I just thought of myself and my gang affiliates, what I would
call if I was out, homies. Basically selling drugs and keeping money
in my pocket.

*What was the mind-set of your home boys when you were gang-
banging?*
Basically, the same thing, except, you know, you see all my
homies was older than me, so theirs was probably a little different
because they were probably on a different level than me a little bit.
They was at the same gang level as me but their age was different,
20, 21. I was a "Little G." I was caught up in it. My family was in
it, so really that's what had me caught up in it. I'd be around my
family every day and they gang-bang. So I gang-bang, too, just
because they gang-bangin'. I think if I was out right now, I'd be
shot or dead. Six feet deep or somethin' because I'd be doin' some
hard bangin'. I'm sorta glad I'm in here, 'cause, uh, you know what
I'm sayin'? I got you to come to. You know? And you been helpin'
me out since I been in here. And, uh, my family would help me
out. You know what I'm sayin'?

How did being in a gang make you feel?
It made me feel good. But now I realize it ain't shit. I ran my
own life, got to smoke weed, sell drugs, drove my own car, know
what I'm sayin'? High roller, had all kinds of girls, had a good
name, know what I'm sayin'? Got a sayin', "Life in the fast lane
ain't nothin' like. Fast money and girls ain't nothin' funny." Know
what I'm sayin'?

Had a lot of freedom, too, huh?
Yeah. Lot of freedom. Do what I want to.

How did you feel about violence and weapons when you were banging?

I liked the shootin' guns and fightin' every day, know what I'm sayin'? But now I look at it from a different perspective.

How did you feel about gang-banging in relation to your family? Did you think about what could happen to them with you gang-banging?

Nope. Basically, I'll rephrase that. I thought about one person in my family and that was my sister 'cause she was the one takin' care of me. And I didn't want no trouble to come to her through me stayin' with her and everything, so I stay away from her house as much as I can.

How did you feel about girls when you were gang-banging?

Nothin. I called them bitches, broads, hos (whores), whatever. Know what I'm sayin'? To me it was just, uh, get a girl, fuck 'em, leave 'em alone.

What was your typical day like when you were gang-banging?

I woke up with some weed in my hand, left from the house, went to my what you would call my G's house, my big homie. In my olive/gold deuce. Go to his house, kick it, go get a sack, go on the streets and hustle. Hustle daily, every day, 'til that night come. Then I'm gonna party. I'm gonna kick it 'til about eleven. The party do not start 'til eleven or twelve. We gonna kick it. Every day routine. If there ain't no party, you go to your cousin's or your homies or somethin' where you can go kick it, whatever.

How did you feel about school?

I didn't go to school. I went to school until about the eighth grade. Meaning that I went to learn. But I did go to school to the ninth and tenth grade just to socialize. School, I didn't feel too good about it. I just wanted to do my own thing.

How did you feel about drugs? Did you sell any? What was your drug of choice?

Dope? Nah. Didn't use it. All I did was sell it. But weed? I liked the weed. Know what I'm sayin'? Beer? It ain't really no...yeah, it's a drug! Alcohol, beer. But that's about it. But all the other drugs, I just sold them.

Who were your role models? Why did you consider them such?
My "Big G," my cousin, Albert and the people from my set. And my sister! Do not get me wrong. My sister, too. I wasn't paying no attention to her. Know what I'm sayin'? She led a good straight life, you know. She was somewhat my role model.

SALEEM, 17

(Adjudicated for four counts of attempted murder and several assaults)

What was your mind-set when you were gang-banging?
A devious mind. I didn't really care about nobody except me. Just cared about the money, the set, you know. I was just being crazy.

What was the mind-set of your home boys when you were gang-banging?
They was the same as me. But, you know, we had sorta, I'd say, a little bit of care for each other, you know, 'cause we was all in the same set. But if it came down to it, it was everybody for theyselves.

How did being in a gang make you feel?
Powerful.

What do you mean?
Like, control. You had control over a lot of stuff. Like control over havin' money. Control over other people. You the one with the gun, so you got the power. In your hands. You can control people.

How did you feel about violence and weapons when you were banging?
It was fun because you know, you get your adrenaline going, and you get to talk about what you did. It's just funny when you look back on it because you ain't got caught for nothin'. But when you get caught, it's a different story.

So you looked at violence and weapons as a just part of being in the gang?
Yeah.

How did you feel about gang-banging in relation to your family? Did you think about what could happen to them with you gang-banging?

Most of my family is in gangs except my mom. My grandma did it. You know, like the older people, my dad, brother, sister. One of my nephews, cousins, aunties—they all in gangs.

How did you feel about girls when you were gang-banging?
Man! I didn't think nothin' of 'em except, you know, can I say it?

Yeah.
Bitches. Just something to fuck.

What was your typical day like when you were gang-banging?
Wake up, put on some khakis, throw on a t-shirt, lay your hat on a flag, with your gun, call da homies up. Go get some drank, some bud, go out, roll some dice, kick it at a park, whatever. Basically that's it. Go to sleep.

How did you feel about school?
I didn't go to school.

Why not?
Because every time I'd go to school I got kicked out for fightin', gang-related activities, carryin' guns.

Did you care about getting your education?
Not at the time. The only thing I needed to know then was how to count money.

How did you feel about drugs? Did you sell any? What was your drug of choice?
Sold drugs, drunk alcohol, smoked weed . . . about it.

Who were your role models? Why did you consider them such?
My role models? One of them was Tony Montana. Scarface.

From the movie?
Yeah, I wanted to be like him. I wanted to. But now, I do not want to. I'm locked up.

So your role models were drug dealers or other gang members?
Yeah. Gangster-type people.

LEWIS, 16

(Adjudicated for attempted murder)

What was your mind-set when you were gang-banging?
I didn't care about nobody. I didn't care about myself, my family.
I didn't care what happened to me. I didn't care if I hurt somebody.

What was the mind-set of your home boys when you were gang-banging?
It was all basically, just us and nobody. Somebody crossed us
wrong, it was just they ass, you know? We didn't care about
nobody but ourselves.

How did being in a gang make you feel?
It made me feel stronger. It made me feel wanted. You know. I
had somebody there that cared about me, so I thought. You know
what I'm sayin'? Just made me feel wanted, you know, like a family.

How did you feel about violence and weapons when you were banging?
I glorified that a lot, you know. When it was happenin' it was
fun, you know. You had weapons so they gave you power, you
know. You pull out a gun and you can see the fear in they face,
you know. It just gave you a lot of power.

How did you feel about gang-banging in relation to your family? Did you think about what could happen to them with you gang-banging?
My family knew I was bangin' and everything. Sometimes they
would try to talk to me and tell me, you know, I shouldn't be doin'
it because I gonna bring that stuff back to the house, this and that.
People be tryin' to git me, but I wouldn't really be listening to that
'cause you know there was a lot of fame, and just too much power,
you know? I didn't really listen to what they were sayin'. I wasn't
really thinkin' about what could happen to them, you know, until
later on.

How did you feel about girls when you were gang-banging?
I didn't care about girls. I mean girls was just, like, a material
thang, you know. Just use 'em for they money, sex . . . it didn't
really matter. If I could sell 'em, fine.

What was your typical day like when you were gang-banging?
I'd wake up about twelve, sometimes one. Before I even get dressed, I'd call the Willie Man, get some bud, and uh, I end up cookin' me somethin' to eat 'cause I got the munchies, call one a my home boys to find out what they doing that day. Or they came over, then they bring some drank, you know. Find out what girls is available, you know, to go kick with, have sex with. Just basically wakin' up and goin' to sleep high.

How did you feel about school?
I didn't care about school. The only thing I went to school for was to clown. To act crazy and make people look stupid. But that's all I was doin' — makin' myself look stupid.

How did you feel about drugs?
That was, I mean, seemed like that was my life, you know. If I wasn't high, I was really livin', you know, in the real world. I didn't really want to face the real world. Bein' high was my life.

Did you ever sell drugs?
Yep.

What were your drugs of choice? What did you like to do the most?
Weed and alcohol.

Who were your role models?
My older Gs and home boys. My older home boys that did mix me into the hood, you know, and bring me up in the streets, you know. No role models in my family, you know. I didn't look up to them because I didn't want to look up to them.

RONNIE, 19

(Adjudicated for murder)

What was your mind-set when you were gang-banging?
My mind-set? Just, you know, live day-by-day. You know, just very sick livin'. You know. My needs. Or I should say, my wants. Just get my money. And if that means robbin' somebody or sellin' dope or lyin' to my mother or stealin', you know, whatever, I'd do it.

What was the mind-set of your home boys when you were gang-banging? Was it the same as yours?

Yep. You know, like that old sayin', misery loves company? They was my home boys 'cause we all thought the same and did the same thing.

Describe what your typical routine day would be like for you when you were banging from the moment you got up.

When I got up? First of all I would come home drunk, so I got up with a hangover. Mom would probably yell at me because I'm gettin' up too late or whatever. I'd iron my clothes up. My clothes would be gang clothes also. I'd crease them on up. I'd be wearing my gang's colors from head to toe. I'd have a hat on. I'd make sure my hat was very creased up, you know, and all of it was clean because I guess you can say your hat represent the whole gang. A lot of gang members take pride in they hats, you know. If they knock your hat off, that's a major challenge. I'd have shoelaces in my gang's colors.

I lived in a rival gang's neighborhood. That's much different than in L.A. But we all grew up together before we had gangs in Portland. Anyway, I liked wearing my outfit from one side of town to the other just to claim my so-called "hood," you know. Basically I'd kick it there, you know. I'd get in some cars and we'd go around and do some dirt, go on some beer runs, shot at people. I'd go over there to the hood, sell dope, and basically stay there all day. Come home and be drunk again and wake up with a hangover all over again. It was just a daily, everyday thing.

How did being in a gang make you feel?

It made me feel, you know, powerful, you know, and ruthless. My gang name was Little Insane Patches, you know, because I used to hang around a bigger dude named Patches, so I put that name on my hat. I had to act out my name so I became that word.

How did you feel about violence and weapons when you were banging?

It was a normal day thing, to me, you know. I'm small, so you know, I'm gonna have me a gat, a gun, of choice, you know. I didn't care how big it was because I was gonna handle it. That was part of the image, you know, to be insane, you know how to handle it. Small and everything, you know. But if I didn't have a gun, I had a hammer, or a bat or something. You know what I'm sayin?

Something that will hurt somebody, you know, if they get out-of-pocket or if I have to defend myself, you know? Or fight the rival gang.

How accessible were weapons to you and your homies?
Shoot, man! I could go to the hood and get a gun, probably in five minutes.

How would you do that?
I'd tell somebody like one of the bigger Gs or whatever, or somebody who had a lot of guns, that "Hey, such-and-such, I need a gun." And he's like,"How much money you got?" or "What kind do you want? How many bullets, you know, do you want to carry?" Whatever, and I'd tell that person. And he'd say, "All right, I'll see what I can do," or "I got one right now," or he'd hook me up with someone else who would want to sell it. Or we would go do a jack move and rob, you know, somebody that have a lot of guns.

How did you feel about girls when you were gang-banging?
It's like, to me, I really didn't beat on a female because that was another issue with me, growing up seeing my father do that to my mother. So, although there were times I got out of hand and did do that to females, but basically I thought of females as just, you know, the b-i-t-c-h word. You know what I'm sayin'? I knew what the b-i-t-c-h word mean. You know what I'm sayin'? You know, the basic female dog. That's the only term. But it's like, again, misery likes company, and I feel that you're a gang member, you're gonna attract gang girls, know what I'm sayin'? And part of their initiation is gettin', you know, ran up in. So I didn't have no respect for females, you know, like I do now.

How did you feel about gang-banging in relation to your family? Did you think about what could happen to them with you gang-banging? Did it matter to you?
It mattered sometimes, and sometime it didn't. It mattered when I came home and got that big lecture. My mom didn't approve of it at all. I can recall at times she snatched me out of cars plenty of times with my so-called homies. And they all knew my mom didn't play! They all told me, "Man, your mom do not play!" And she's just the type, you know? She tell me she's not gonna tolerate it. You know? But it's like, the other family members, you know, who was' kinda hooked up in sellin' drugs and stuff. They knew I was into that but they really didn't pressure me. They would

give me little hints and stuff, you know. But for the other family members I had respect for I would play Jekyll and Hyde. When I'd get around one particular family member or whatever, I would portray that real positive nephew or real positive cousin or grandson. I learned at a real early age from the streets, how to manipulate and how to play that front role. Know what I'm sayin'? But to sum it up, my family didn't approve of it all, you know?

Did you care what could happen to your family because of your banging?

It didn't matter, you know, to me because it's like, I had so much stuff going inside my mind, my heart, whatever, you know? It's like I didn't care, you know? My mother tried to tell me it's threatening her and my little brother and the rest of the family, whatever, but I didn't care, you know? It went in one ear and right out the other.

How did you feel about school?

I didn't like school at all. It was just bottom line, you know? Point blank. I didn't like school at all. The only time I kind of liked the school was, you know to go sell drugs and hang out wit my pa'tners, whatever. And show some girls that I had a lot of money. And try to show that money. You know, a clout move and everything. But academics, you know, and just basically gettin' some knowledge in my head, it was not for me.

How did you feel about drugs? Did you sell any? What was your drug of choice?

I felt that I would never do crack. Know what I'm sayin'? And I didn't do crack. I kind of felt you know, kinda tore up inside, and at the same time I wouldn't care. Because I used marijuana and alcohol. But I felt tore up inside because I saw family members that once had theyself together and stuff, and now there's no pride, you know, livin' off of us, or mom tryin' to help 'em out, or just seein' their kids split up and stuff like that, and seein' how they had to suffer. So I kinda showed a little sympathy when I used to sell drugs in the dope house. I would tell the mothers or the fathers that would bring their kids in the dope house to take the kids somewhere else, you know? That was the child coming out in me. I knew how that kid was feelin'. So if they would take the kid outside the dope house, I'd sell 'em drugs.

What was your favorite drug?

Marijuana and just any kind of alcohol. Any kind. Beer, Mad Dog 20/20, Wild Irish Rose, Cool Breeze, any kind. I didn't care.

Who were your role models?

Pimps, drug dealers, and gang members. And the so-called family members that tried to be role models, it wasn't in a positive sense. They were just negative, talked negative. Verbal abuse, basically.

Common Themes

There are many common themes in the statements of each of these youths. Their stories are similar to the stories of many gangsters and incarcerated youths all around our country. Through their stories, you can see how their value system is totally different from that of mainstream society. Their attitudes and outlook on life supports working with this population as a treatment issue, which requires serious intervention to elicit positive changes in attitudes and behaviors.

If you look a little deeper, you will notice something else. Each of these young men was able to describe the path he took to get where he is. These youths can describe in detail the choices they made, the actions they took, and the people and forces that influenced their actions and decisions.

All of us must recognize the wealth of information that stands before us in each youth we encounter. As they enlighten us with their stories, they also are revealing that they understand many of the things that they must not do, or that they must undo, if they are to live more productive lives when they get out.

In other words, they can see clearly now. Perhaps they did all along. Deep down, they know what not to do. But we still must answer the challenge the one youth put forth: show me a reason not to bang.

4

understanding gang dynamics and culture; how gangs communicate and intimidate: gang graffiti, handsigns, and vernacular

As we have discussed already, youths heavily involved in gang activity have a different mind-set than mainstream society. Actions which would be unthinkable to mainstream society are quite acceptable to them. To understand gangs, it is important to understand their structure and culture.

Street gangs are not as structured as the Mafia. Within a gang, some members have more influence than others, but it is unlikely a top man (godfather or don) is calling the shots.

In gangs, leadership is assumed rather than formally given. There are often many leaders in a "set." Those who demonstrate dominant characteristics, possess a specific criminal skill, have the most status, command the most respect, or initiate many of a gang's criminal behaviors, are the O.G.s. The highest goal among gang-involved youths is to be considered an O.G. Neophyte gangsters are called B.G.s (baby gangsters).

Nicknames or Monikers

One of the first things a gang does with a new member, or B.G., is to give him a new nickname or moniker. The gang generally selects a name that fits the person's stature, physical traits, psychological make-up, or some other characteristic — real, imagined, or desired. Examples include: 8-ball, Little Patches, Glockmaster, Shadow-Loc, N-sane, and Scarface.

Handsigns

A common behavioral thread between Los Angeles' style gangs is the use of handsigns that identify members as part of a particular gang or "set." Flashing a handsign to another within a "set" is an expression of bonding and unity. When done in the presence of a rival, it is intended as a sign of gross disrespect for the other's "set." When combined with a crazy look or stare, it is an unmistakable challenge and a threat to inflict serious damage.

Tattoos

Tattoos are a common communication device for gang-involved youths. Tattoos may range from crude etchings of the individual gang member's moniker or a small symbol such as a cross or teardrop to more elaborate artwork and figures, such as chains, hearts, or weapons. Tattoos are often on conspicuous parts of the body, such as fingers, neck, legs, arms, or even the cheeks or forehead. Often, the nature and location of tattoos express irreversible commitment to the gang.

Eye contact

In the gang culture, it is a sign of weakness not to make eye contact with someone, particularly a member of a rival gang or "set." Gang members will stare each other down with their craziest, hardest look in a show of wills.

Gang graffiti

People across the country are increasingly aware of spray-painted words, letters, and symbols across formerly blank walls of buildings in their communities. This graffiti bears little resemblance to the "John loves Mary" that was carved into trees or written in the stalls of restrooms a generation ago.

The markings are cryptic, coded messages — not intended for widespread comprehension. This graffiti might be the work of a lone "tagger," but more often, it is a gang's way of warning rival gangs of their intention to claim and control the building and its vicinity. A gang "set" may conduct a form of "roll call" on a wall or building, with each member writing his moniker on a designated wall in their turf. Trouble may ensue if a rival gang subsequently lines out one or more names on that wall, an act considered to be a promise to kill the persons whose names are lined out.

To intimidate a particular rival, a gang may write the rival's name or moniker on a wall, then draw a line across it. They may write the name and the number of their state's penal code section that refers to homicide. In California, that section number is 187. Even outside of California, "187" may be used by "sets" founded by transplanted California gangsters, or by youths styling themselves after California-based gangs.

It is common to see the name or moniker of a slain gang member written on a wall with "RIP" before or after it. If a rival gang scratches out that tribute, gang experts know there is real trouble brewing. Police and gang-intervention specialists constantly strive to increase their ability to recognize and understand these messages in the attempt to head off retaliatory violence.

Distinctions Between Work of Taggers and Gang Graffiti

People who deface public property with spray paint under cover of darkness and disappear before they are caught are commonly referred to as "taggers." Taggers use spray paint, chalk and other media to express themselves, often artistically, on publicly visible property, such as buildings, highway overpasses, public transportation vehicles, and signs. While some taggers work in small groups and are considered gangs because they get together to engage in antisocial and criminal acts of trespass and vandalism, many taggers are individuals who enjoy the rush of excitement that comes from the risk of getting caught and the euphoria of seeing their handiwork in broad daylight. For taggers, the writing or marking is the end in itself.

By contrast, street-gang graffiti is intended to communicate messages about a particular "set's" presence or state of mind. A secondary purpose of street-gang graffiti is to intimidate law-abiding citizens and discourage them from reporting criminal activity they see to the authorities. Not sure who has defaced the property, citizens often do not know from whom they might expect retaliation. It is risky to use just one indicator to decide if you have gang activity going on in your institution or neighborhood, but graffiti is certainly an act worth investigating.

Section II

breaking through gang mentality; getting a gang intervention program underway

5

the committed facilitator: the cornerstone of any successful gang-intervention program

The most important figure in any effective gang-intervention program is the facilitator. Rather than forming enabling relationships that allow the youths to continue their well-developed manipulations, the facilitator must be able to establish caring relationships that empower the participants to live responsible lives. Facilitators must be strong, determined, and committed individuals with an authentic understanding of the culture. Additionally, facilitators must have a relentless commitment to helping young men make the necessary changes and adjustments. Facilitators can come from any race or be of either gender. Any person committed to working with gang-affected youths can apply the strategies we have outlined in this book. What matters far more than ethnicity is a facilitator's ability to demonstrate his or her convictions and commitments to the youths.

When a youth believes he is dealing with a person who has taken the time and put in the effort to really understand him and that this person genuinely cares about him, the youth is in the process of dealing with his mind-set and issues. When that person shows him realistic options and choices that are within his reach and within his own control, he is much more likely to trust both the person and his own abilities. He will be much more willing to believe that he can be more than a drug dealer, a hustler, or a gangster. Remember, most gang-involved youths already have demonstrated the capacity for fierce loyalty. It is impossible to overstate the long-term benefit of having such loyalty channeled into the positive peer culture of your program.

We had a young man named Reggie in our positive peer group. Reggie's mother actively supported our program. Shortly before Reggie completed his eighteen-month stay at our facility, his father was released from prison. His father had a difficult time adjusting to life back in the community. Frustrated, he went on a drinking binge. He became verbally abusive and threatened to physically abuse Reggie's mother. She feared he would do something that would send him back to prison on a parole violation.

In desperation, she called this author at midnight, frightened and concerned. She put her husband on the phone, and we talked for a few minutes. Understanding the depth of his frustration, the author promised that one of his associates and he would come to their house to talk.

While he vented with us, Reggie's mother went to her sister's house for safety. Ultimately, we were able to defuse the situation and avoided the need for police action. We also were able to get some of our community partners to make some resources and services available to Reggie's dad to help him regain his confidence and sense of purpose.

Our response to this situation certainly benefitted Reggie's parents. We kept his mother safe and his father out of prison. But we also accomplished much more — it further strengthened the trust and confidence Reggie's family had in our program, assuring us of the alliance we would need to sustain long after Reggie's release from our facility. Reggie's already strong motivation to be a positive role model in our program was strengthened when he heard what we had done for his father.

Service of this sort, well above and beyond the standard job description, but well within the call of duty, is what a successful gang-intervention program must provide. We do advise you to exercise caution in situations like the one we described here since it could be dangerous. You have to know the family as well as the youth involved. You may need to call 911 to ensure the safety of everyone involved. In Reggie's case, we knew the family and felt we were not putting anyone at risk. Please exercise good judgment before acting in a potentially dangerous situation.

Within the correctional facility, it may be necessary to return to the campus in the middle of the night when notified of a volatile situation. It will mean so much more to those involved, directly and peripherally, to see that you respond when the situation is brewing or hot and help resolve it, rather than coming in the next morning, reading an incident report and then reacting to second-hand accounts. Doing this is another way of "walking your talk," and manifesting your commitment to the ultimate goal. It also strengthens the commitment of support staff to see your passion for your mission.

intervention strategies to help gang-involved youths see the need to turn their lives around

Keys to a Successful Program

The goals of the Minority Youth Concerns Program at the MacLaren Youth Correctional Facility are prevention, intervention, and empowerment. These three elements are the key to a comprehensive, successful program.

Prevention helps youth who are fascinated by gangs, but who are not actually involved with them. We show them reasons why they must decide not to jump into gang involvement.

Intervention helps gang-involved youth and those on the fringes of gangs see the need to redirect their lives and to get out of the gang.

Empowerment provides youth with the power to take responsibility for their lives and provides strategies for becoming successful, productive people.

Once a trusting relationship has been established, some frank, one-on-one talk is in order. At the MacLaren Youth Correctional Facility, we ask three questions in our screening process:

1. Can you think for yourself?

2. Can you tell the difference between fantasy and reality?

3. Will you open up your mind to the information we offer in this program?

When a young man answers affirmatively to each questions, we tell him confidently, "We won't have to try to drag you out of a gang. You will see the need yourself."

Curriculum

We have a specific curriculum for a treatment approach to gang intervention. The topic order and format varies to fit the dynamics of a particular individual or group, but we make every effort to cover all of the following subjects as part of our intervention strategy.

1. Orientation

2. Reflections on the realities gangsters disregard: the lure of fast money, the human toll of gang violence, and the criminal justice system

3. Ethnic on ethnic crime: who is the real enemy?

4. Role models: appropriate and inappropriate

5. Peer pressure, true friends, and independent thinking

6. Anger management, conflict resolution, and mediation

7. Self-knowledge through historical awareness

8. Racism and prejudice

9. Values clarification

10. Individual responsibility: self-determination and goal setting

11. Maximum benefits from a minimum-wage job

12. Personal growth as a life-long mission

13. Job opportunities and entrepreneurship

14. Child rearing

A session may span three or four group meetings and dozens of individual encounters since there are many subtopics encompassed in each major subject. We use a full armory of resources in pursuing these objectives, including large group discussions, video presentations, and role-plays. Most important and effective is straight, frank talk, "right-word," and man-to-man lectures by the staff. We share the knowledge we have gained from our own experience as well as the experience of others whose lives have been affected by their involvement with gangs and crime. We have small group discussions so young men can participate and interact on a more intimate level. And, of course, we take time to work with each youth one-on-one in individual counseling to see how they reacted to prior group sessions. These interactions allow us to tailor our approach to the personal and psychological needs of each youth in our program.

"Right-word" does not just come from staff. We regularly bring in guest speakers from the community, family members, career people, justice system officials, parole officers, and former gangsters. Each guest contributes to the education and motivation of our young men. The fact that these people would take time out of their lives to visit our participants and to offer encouragement affirms the idea that their lives are worth saving and redirecting.

Preparing for the Inevitable Resistance

When orienting young men to the program and encouraging them to get involved, we realize that youths initially may join for reasons significantly different from the reasons we wish they had joined. The majority initially may have entered the program with no real intent of discontinuing their drug selling and gang involvement. They may participate for a chance to get together and see their "homeboys" or to project their gang image onto their rivals who also may be in the program. They may want to use the program to look good to authorities in the hope that their participation will help them get paroled.

In any program, including ours, we understand these young men may enter the program with the belief that being in a gang and selling drugs is the best, if not only, way to gain love, respect, and financial security. Because of this belief, these young men will bombard you with rationalizations for continuing their gang lifestyle.

During these early stages, the young men are sure to test your knowledge and commitment. You will not be dealing with Boy Scouts. And there will be times when you wonder why you are trying to help these troubled young men. It is critical to have the strength and endurance necessary to rise to the challenges gang-affiliated youths will present.

You must respond effectively to the excuses and questions they will throw at you in defense of their antisocial behavior. If you want to stand any chance of getting these youths to take a look at the issues they need to explore while internalizing the motivation to change, your responses must show that you care about them, know what you are talking about, can be trusted, and are worth listening to. This is no small order, but without accomplishing these things, they will not listen to you.

Forcing them to leave the gang will fail. The goal in the orientation stage should not be to overpower the youths' wills, but to get them thinking. You must be prepared, not with canned, pat answers, but with information and questions that provoke the young men to reexamine the limitations they have accepted for their future.

In any gang-intervention program, there will be guys so committed to their gangs that they will make statements to you such as the following:

- "I'm going to be a gangster for life."

- "I'm willing to die for my set and my homeboys."

- "I'm not afraid of going to prison."

This is the kind of mentality we face. We are not there to battle them and drag them out of their former lifestyles. We are there to help them follow through on their agreement to participate in the program and to consider the information presented to them. Hopefully, at the conclusion of the program, the desire for change will be complete.

Session One: Orientation

In this session we focus on:

- Introducing the adult facilitators and students

- Explaining the program's importance

- Outlining the rules of conduct

- Providing a detailed list of expectations

- Outlining the components of the program available to students (job readiness sessions, small group meetings, tutoring, and so forth)

- Receiving student input

- Holding a question and answer period

We meet individually with each young man to explain the program and to secure his commitment to cooperate before our first group meeting. We use the first group session to orient the program group and to let them know we expect them to be open to the information presented. We also discuss ground rules for maintaining order in the program. These rules include not interrupting others, not playing around, not displaying gang behaviors, and not putting others down.

In the first session, we make sure all the youth understand the nature of the program. We tell them that participation is voluntary. We remind everyone to stay focused and insist that the rules of conduct we have established are upheld. We say something to the effect of the following: "We are talking about issues relevant to your futures — that are literally life and death issues, and if you are here, we expect you to be attentive and involved."

We also share information about why we put the program together and share information about ourselves as facilitators. We ask the young men to introduce themselves and to share their histories and present mind-sets with the rest of the group. We encourage them to be as honest as possible about their current feelings about gang involvement.

Session Two: Reflecting on the Realities Gangsters Disregard

In this session we focus on:

- The lure of fast money

- The impact of the criminal justice system

- The impact of drugs and alcohol, in a culturally specific manner

- The influence of the media, including gangster rap music and violence on film

We begin this session by giving the young men the opportunity to express their feelings about themselves before and during their gang involvement. Many of the participants can tell us what attracted them to gangs, either because they still consider themselves gangsters loyal to their "sets," or because they are not far removed from that mind-set. We encourage them to speak freely about their reasons for choosing gang involvement and to describe in vivid detail what it was like to be willing to die for their "sets." We let them talk about how gangs meet their primary needs for love, support, belonging, money, and other indications of status. In this phase, we are careful to affirm the universal needs they tried to meet through gang involvement. We let them speak for as long as we can elicit frank and authentic reflections on why they became gangsters.

After orientation, we have the group take a look at gang involvement with additional information they may not have previously taken into account, to open up their minds to the true, negative reality of gang involvement. When young men are out there running with gangs, they only focus on the exhilaration, protection, and other benefits of being in gangs. In here, we can slow them down and have them take a long, hard look at things they do not ordinarily examine until it is too late. In other words, we expand their perspective and look at the whole picture. We take a look at the impact that their gang activity has on them, their communities, and others.

Reality One: the Lure of Fast Money

Most of our young men have not been thinking about the future. They need to expand their horizon and see the long-range effect of the gang lifestyle. Our part is to let them open up so we can give them the true picture of gang-involvement.

One of the biggest issues is the young men's desire for immediate gratification. The notion of gradual, sometimes slow, results is often quite alien to a young man who has been used to making $500 to $1,000 a day selling crack cocaine. They know that by selling drugs or robbing somebody, they get money right away to buy clothes, jewelry, cars, and other items. We would have no credibility with them if we were to tell them that they cannot make money selling drugs or doing other dangerous, illegal things. Instead, we show them the whole picture and allow them to draw their own conclusions from a broader, deeper knowledge-base.

Again, our purpose is not to tell them that they cannot make money selling drugs, to disagree or disapprove of them, but to say, "Yes, you can make that kind of money, but take an honest look at other factors that go along with it you might not have considered."

Points we make include:

- *You are making money and acquiring your material things off the suffering of others.*

A lot of gang activity involves battling other gangs for control of areas to sell crack cocaine and other illegal substances. We point out that most of the people they are "jacking" or selling drugs to are people who live in their own community—their neighbors and people of their own ethnic background.

We show videotapes of news accounts, documentaries, and other productions, which illustrate the impact drugs have on the people they sell to and innocent third parties, such as babies born addicted to crack. We show a videotape of a woman who is addicted to crack cocaine, gets pregnant, continues to use drugs, and gives birth to a crack-addicted baby. We show them the suffering and other complications that the newborn endures. We have them consider their role in such tragedies.

We show them articles and other sources detailing how drugs are physically, emotionally, and mentally detrimental. We also show them the impact drug houses have on the tranquillity of a neighborhood and on property values. Once these realities register with them, we ask the students to consider what it means to do that to their own people.

- *Money acquired through criminal means can be enjoyed only for a very short time.*

We have our participants acknowledge that although the money comes fast, it goes fast because they are not investing the money. They are not letting it work for them because they have not gone to school and learned about business investments.

- *Even the high rollers do not last.*

We use real-life examples of people our youths know to make the point that there is no long-term success or comfort as a gangster; the higher one ascends in the world of crime and drugs, the more certain one is to have it all eventually come crashing down.

One of our most effective examples is a man who was a big-time drug dealer in Northeast Portland. He appeared to have it made, with his Rolls Royce and custom-made Corvette, jewelry, gold, and big wads of money in his pockets. This man rented a condo in an upscale part of Portland. With no apparent job, his neighbors became suspicious of his lavish lifestyle. It did not take them long to figure out what was going on and to contact the police who set up an undercover operation.

He depended on people of doubtful character, at best, to sell drugs for him. When they got arrested, they did not hesitate to snitch on him to get out of trouble, to shorten their sentences, or to otherwise help themselves. When the condo owners learned they had a drug dealer on their premises, they did not hesitate to evict him.

Today, the man is serving a twenty-year prison term in a federal facility. He entered prison in his twenties. He will be more than forty-years old when he is released, provided he is not killed in prison. He had used his cars, jewelry, gold, and big wads of money to lure people into a criminal lifestyle. All of the material things he accumulated were seized by the federal government under drug forfeiture laws. In prison, he has nothing but state-issued clothes.

- *The moments of pleasure and status come at a very high price.*

The real life example just cited serves to illustrate an equally important reality — what looks like "livin' large" with fast money and other fruits of criminal enterprise is anything but living comfortably. The drug dealer attracted people who had no problem trying to steal what he had. He probably got little sleep and kept a gun under his pillow, never knowing who might show up to harm and rob him. In fact, he was robbed on several occasions. Once he was kidnapped and shot twice in the stomach. He lived a life of paranoia, fearing people on both sides of the law. Because many of our young men have heard of this person, his story is convincing proof that his high-roller's life was anything but carefree.

Our participants are used to living in the moment, and we need to teach them to have a future-oriented perspective. We stress laying a foundation now for a comfortable future. We show them that no matter where they come from, if they take on responsibility and work hard, they can have material things and success. We help them see that if they live honestly, they will have more time with their families, and they will have the personal freedom they do not have now. We tell them that they can live longer lives and have the comforts of life that cannot be taken away.

To get them to rethink the fast-money lifestyle, we point out that they are expending enough energy on the streets to have the success they want, but they will have little to show for the sacrifices they made because they were spending their energies in the wrong manner. We may tell them the following:

> You are out there selling drugs, counting money, hustling. If you put that energy into positive endeavors, you'd be successful. You have to work hard to achieve it, but in the long run you will be able to live a longer life, be with your family, and have your personal liberty.

An example we use quite a bit is a character that Wesley Snipes played in the popular movie *New Jack City*. This intelligent young man grew up in the "hood" and saw no options other than hustling and selling drugs. Growing up in a poor family, surrounded by a lot of violence and drugs, his role models were gangsters and drug dealers. He wanted to be a high roller. He grew up, sold drugs, and created an empire with his own office and staff. His organization was as solid as any successful business. He was the CEO of his business with underlings doing his bidding. But his business wasn't legitimate.

He preyed on his own community. He did not have the respect or love of the people because they knew what he represented. The only respect he had was from other dealers, and many of them were scheming to take his place. He led a paranoid life. Ultimately, he was killed by a community member who was fed up with his drug dealing and destructive effect on the community. He lived large, but despite the cars, money, and women, he died at a very young age. All his material things were lost and the community did not miss him one bit. What kind of legacy did he leave to his family and community? A negative one. He was a drug dealer and a statistic.

We ask our participants to consider how this character's charisma might have impacted on his community if he had pursued an education, worked hard, and set long- and short-term goals.

Even growing up in harsh conditions, with his energy and charisma, he could have been successful at whatever he wanted to do. If only he had been encouraged to turn in a different direction, he could have lived a long, full life with the respect of the community, with a family and children of his own following in his footsteps. However, he never saw, or considered any other possibilities. We want our guys to see that there are other options.

We have too many salvageable young men ignoring life's options and accepting the idea that the only thing they are destined to be is drug dealers and gang-bangers. We remind them there are still many young men and young women growing up in the same environments and communities who are not joining gangs or selling drugs. They face the same kinds of pressures, but they are going to school, being responsible, and trying to achieve something in their lives.

Many of these young men call such people "squares, suckers, and preppies." We turn the tables on them, because the ones they call "squares and suckers" are the ones laying foundations for their futures. They are the ones who will have freedom, who will be able to take their families on vacations, who will have self-esteem and self-respect. They will benefit their communities.

By contrast, the only respect the drug dealers are going to get will come from people who are hypnotized by that kind of lifestyle. Their life will be very short. They either will die young or end up incarcerated.

Many young men will say, "I'm a gangster for life. I do not care about going to prison. I'll die for my homeboys." But they are the very ones unhappy about their treatment in our institution. They complain about poor treatment by the staff. They have a hard time relating to their peers. They have to shower together and do other things at specific times chosen by someone else. Yet, they continue to live lifestyles that are destined either to keep them in such controlled environments or to result in their deaths at a young age — if they do not waste away first, strung out on drugs and alcohol.

We tell them that a young person with limited education, few skills, and little or no positive support is unlikely to get the kind of jobs necessary to achieve self-sufficiency. "You're likely to be frustrated and to surround yourself with other people in bad circumstances. You'll probably abuse drugs and alcohol, sell drugs, and eventually end up a statistic and part of the system. So, who are the 'squares and suckers'?" We suggest they are not the ones who are going on and getting their education, saying no to gangs, setting goals, and trying to achieve them. They sound like people who are trying to be somebody with their lives regardless of their circumstances.

Another example that backs up our contention that selling drugs is always going to be nothing more than a short-term proposition is a Hispanic drug dealer in Northeast Portland. He was making hundreds of thousands of dollars each month with a tightly knit group. One of his most trusted and reliable men was arrested. The police tried to get this fellow to turn on his friend, the drug dealer. They offered to reduce charges if he would agree to be an informant.

He agreed and gathered and relayed enough information on the dealer's operation to lead to a search warrant. This leader had all kinds of money, jewelry, and cars. He was arrested, charged, and convicted. At twenty-five, he was sentenced to a federal penitentiary. We show a videotape featuring the drug dealer in which he reminisces about "living large." He says that if he had it to do over again, he would make different choices about his lifestyle, because all he has for the next twenty-five years are the memories. He is going to lose his twenties, thirties, and forties sitting out those years in federal prison.

Many of our gang-involved youths say they do not care about prison. The truth is, they have no idea what adult corrections is like. We point out what it is really like to live the prime of your life behind bars, cut off from women, family, and from any kind of social life. We ask them to name the things that bother them about juvenile corrections. They usually mention missing their families, lack of privacy, lack of vacations, and missing family milestones such as births and weddings and even funerals. They do not like the food or lack of privileges. We point out that all this exists in adult corrections, as well. We say:

> So in a year here, you've missed out on the birth of your brother and your sister's wedding. You didn't get to go to your friend's funeral. Your girlfriend is seeing somebody else. What do you think happens in ten or twenty years? How much do you think you'll miss out on during those times? If you have a child, you'll miss the child growing up. Maybe he or she will be a baby when you come in. By the time you get out, that baby will be grown, and you'll have missed the whole thing. Maybe your mother will die, and you won't have had any time to do anything with her, to show her you could make something of your life.

We also point out that life in the adult corrections system is a harder life than it is at the MacLaren Youth Correctional Facility. There is more violence, more sexual exploitation, less treatment, and fewer privileges.

We follow people who traveled the route some of our students say they want to take — the way of fast money. We show them the reality of the situation. We let them know they can overcome the conditions of their environment if they are willing to work and make sacrifices.

We stress that becoming legitimately rich involves a process which requires time. We point out that young people in their late teens should not expect to drive BMWs or Mercedes Benzes, and that the value system that expects such things so early in life is out of whack. There are no shortcuts to lasting wealth.

It is very important for our young men to hear from people their own age who have stayed on the right side of the law and who are making steady progress toward careers and independent living. We invite such young people in and ask them to tell, in their own words, about the sacrifices they are making to have a secure financial and personal future. Such real-life examples are very important elements in getting these young men to reassess the assumptions that underlie their lifestyle choices. It is virtually impossible to demonstrate this new value system to these young men without real-life examples.

Reality two: The Human Toll of Gang Violence

Drive-by shootings — shooting up someone's house or firing into a crowd of people — are often impersonal, unthinking acts, done with little or no thought given to the likelihood that someone may be hit. In this session, we ask the participants to take a close look at this gang activity and to consider how often this type of violence produces innocent victims, young children, and elderly people who happen to be in the wrong place at the wrong time.

We also have them look at the personal costs of this violence. We show them pictures of people who have died or who have been seriously injured by drive-by shootings. Some young men are under the mistaken notion that a person, once shot, dies right away. We let them know of the slow, agonizing deaths some suffer. We show them photographs of unfortunate people who have survived a gun wound but are confined forever to a wheelchair or who suffered brain damage and never will be able to function on their own again.

Our discussions are frank, explicit, and based on real-life experiences. We offer forensic information, photos, videos, and literature that clearly reveal what a bullet does to human flesh and internal organs.

Our examination of the consequences of gang activity continues with a look at how a person's death affects more than the person whose young life was taken. We show them a funeral that illustrates how the shooting affected everyone who knew and loved the individual. We show them photos and literature about the grieving family members and friends. We try to get them to see the humanity in every person.

In group, we may bring in people from the community who were victims of violence and ask them to talk about how it felt to be attacked. We ask them to describe the physical, emotional, and psychological difficulties they have struggled with in trying to overcome their experiences. We help them understand that even when a victim is fortunate enough to survive a shooting or some other violent act, he may be left handicapped or impaired, physically and mentally, and unable to enjoy the quality of life he or she once had.

Sometimes, we bring in groups of parents whose young children are involved in gangs and have them talk about the impact their children's decision has had on their families — the fear they create for the safety of everyone within their household and the concern that their child may be killed any night. Such guests bring the students face-to-face with the ramifications of violence that they had not seriously considered before.

We help them see that killing a rival not only ends his life, but affects everyone who loves the victim. We have groups view videos of funerals showing parents, aunts, and grandparents who did not think of the deceased as a gangster, but as part of their flesh and blood.

Reality Three: The Criminal Justice System

After the students consider the impact their gang activity may have on others, we shift the focus to the criminal justice system and explain to them that by deciding to run with a gang and engage in gang activity, each of them is deciding to have a file with his name on it opened somewhere in the system. We show them how they can become trapped in a vicious cycle of incarceration, parole, and rein-carceration — especially when they become adults.

We talk about how it feels to do long stretches of time, missing out on vacations and family events like births, weddings, and funerals. There is often less emphasis on treatment in prison, and we point out that they will be surrounded by some very dangerous, negative people. We talk about how others control their lives while they are in prison. We discuss the fact that even when they are out on parole, they still are tethered to someone whose job it is to keep them in line. We compare the differences between the juvenile corrections system and the adult corrections system. We have officials from the adult system talk to the students about what it is like in an adult prison in the United States today.

We talk about certain new laws which are targeting young offenders, such as those that would remand fifteen-year-olds to the adult system, and the new Racketeering Influence and Corrupt Organization Act (RICO), which once was used against the Mafia and now is used against street gangs. We point out that the older they are when they are in the system, the harder it is to get out.

It is hard enough for average law-abiding persons to make it. If they have limited skills, and limited job opportunities, it is extra hard to make it carrying the label of convict, over and above that of gang member.

To present this reality, we have former gang members come in as guest speakers and talk about how their past gang identity has made the already difficult task of starting their new lives even harder. We also show them reports, news clippings, and other proof that funds for support services to youth offenders are dwindling and face an uncertain future. Such resources may not be available to them when they get out. For this reason, we stress how important it is for them to make the change now while the community and the government are in a position to help them follow through.

Secondly, we show them there are even fewer resources available for adult convicts. We say something such as the following:

> If you do not change, it will become harder to make it outside, and you're more likely to come back — repeatedly. When you're in your early twenties with limited skills and education, what are you going to do? Eventually, even your family will give up on you. You start feeling sorry for yourself. You find friends in the same situation — probably those with drug and alcohol problems. You're not as young

and fresh and optimistic as you were the first time you were released from juvenile detention. You fall for another criminal scheme to get by, and eventually you get popped again. The cycle continues because the thought patterns remain the same.

Many adults want to change, but their self-esteem takes a beating. Unable to get a job at forty, they cannot provide for their families. So, they slip back into the world of alcohol and drugs to escape reality. You only get so many opportunities. You have to take control and recognize what is happening to you. Start planning for your future. Take a direction that allows you to have a future. Too many never do and end up as statistics.

Session Three: Ethnic-on-ethnic Crime: Who Is the Real Enemy?

In this session we focus on:

- Seeing gang activity as genocide

- Showing how gang activity affects families, culture, and communities

- Exploring the human toll of gang violence

- Giving the victim a face: developing victim empathy

During this component of the program, we share statistics on ethnic-on-ethnic crime in the United States and proceed beyond the numbers to the human tragedies they represent.

We show the youth that it is always a two-for-one deal. One young man is killed in a gang-related incident and robbed of a future. His life is gone. The person who killed him probably will be convicted and incarcerated for the majority of his life. In addition, the families who love both young men suffer. A series of acts and retaliations is set in motion. One man's "homeboys" go after another man's "homeboys." They are killing each other over colors and over turf in neighborhoods they do not even own. It is frightening to see young men who will kill someone from a rival gang and feel absolutely no remorse over taking a life and endangering many other lives in the process.

We discuss with them why it has to end and why they should see what it is they really are doing to each other. We show them and discuss the need to develop empathy and love for each other.

The Ku Klux Klan Role-Play

When we give out written assignments, one of the first questions we ask young men is whether they have pride in their race. Most of them say that they do. This is always puzzling considering the fact that most of the people they victimize with violence and drug sales are their own people. Whose family has to deal with the death of a young African-American male? An African-American family. We need to help them see that this conduct is suicidal and genocidal. We have to get them to look at each other as human beings. They must see beyond the colors, the neighborhoods, and learn to see each other without artificial labels of enmity.

We tell our young men that Crips, Bloods, and Hispanic gangs are the answer to the prayers of the Ku Klux Klan and the Aryan Nation. One tool we use to make this point is a role-play exercise in which we stage a meeting of the Ku Klux Klan and have a well-dressed black man accidentally enter the meeting. The Klan hurls epithets at him, calling him every ugly name they can think of. They chase him away, threatening to kill him. They resume their meeting after a few belly-laughs about humiliating the African-American man. Then, another African-American man erroneously enters the room. He, however, is wearing gang attire and carrying rocks of crack cocaine. A couple of Klansmen rise to run him off. But they are stopped by others in the group and told to welcome this intruder as one of them.

They sit him down in the middle of the meeting. They pour him a drink and give him VIP treatment in every way. They ask him to tell them if he feels the same exhilaration they do when they shoot up someone's house and drive off; how exciting it feels to gang-up on an African-American person and beat him up. They show their appreciation to their honored guest by rendering a song, set to country music, featuring a few lines from a rap artist's top selling hit about "hunting down a nigger, fuckin' his bitch, then shooting them both." They put a white cone-shaped hood on his head and ask him to sing the second verse. By this time, the gang member no longer is smiling.

We stop the play at this point and discuss the dramatization. The purpose of this exercise is not to make our young men hate white people, or even the Klan, but to help them see how much their former behavior fit the very objectives and practices of such white supremacists' groups. We also use this time to share with them the statistical evidence of their destructive behavior and its impact on their own people.

The Slaughterhouse Exercise

One of the most effective tools we have for opening the eyes of gang-involved youths is the slaughterhouse exercise. In a large group discussion format, we ask everyone to make believe they are cattle and that the room is a slaughterhouse. Ten young men line up facing a closed door. We then send one of them through the door. On the outside, we hear an agonizing scream coming from the other side of the door, followed by silence. Then we send another one in, and again, we hear a scream followed by silence. We continue sending "cattle" in until only two or three remain.

We stop and discuss what the remaining cattle ought to do and why. Invariably, the youths say that the remaining cattle ought to do whatever they can to get out of there. At the very least, they should not go through the door. In fact, they should do all they could to get out of the room. To do anything less would be suicidal. Why walk voluntarily to certain death?

We return to today's world. We tell them that the closed door is the entry-way into gangs. Again, ten young men line up facing the door. We send in one of them. On the outside, we hear a news reporter from the other side of the door reporting that a young man involved in a gang has been sentenced to twenty years in federal prison for dealing crack cocaine. We send another young man in, and again we hear the news reporter broadcast that another young man has been shot to death by members of a rival gang. We continue sending young men through the door into gang membership, with similar "news accounts" until only two or three remain.

We discuss what those remaining outside the door ought to do and why. Usually, the responses come a little slower, as the young men are not as quick to state the obvious about gang-involvement as they were when they were talking about cattle. Eventually, however, the young men acknowledge that the other young men should not go through the door.

Having elicited such commonsense responses, we discuss the similarities and differences between cattle going to slaughter and young men joining a gang or returning to gang involvement after seeing the information we have shown them. The only clear difference between the two is that cattle are unable to avoid their demise because they are dumb and unable to know the fate awaiting them on the other side of the door. Unlike human beings, they cannot reason. They cannot deliberate. They cannot compare. They do not pass information about the past, present, or future from one to another. Consequently, their actions are the product of either instinct or the domination of their human lords.

The point of the exercise hardly ever is missed. When confronted with the similarities between the conduct of the cattle and that of thousands of human beings marching for certain destruction, the participants are equipped with one more reason for divorcing themselves from the vicious cycle and the death-ridden lifestyle of gang involvement.

The young men usually are more willing to give good, frank advice to a fictional cow than they are to give the sound advice to their younger human brothers. What, if anything, does that say?

Session Four: Role Models—Appropriate and Inappropriate

In this session we focus on:

- Understanding characteristics common to negative role models

- Understanding characteristics common to positive role models

- Learning how to find positive role models

We have our young men take a look at their past role models to see that what looked like a solid, secure, exciting lifestyle may have attracted young people like themselves into the gang lifestyle. We get the fellows to talk about the role models that influenced them as they were growing up. In most instances, they were negative role models: "O.G.s," hustlers, and pimps — people whose status and possessions were gained in ways that usually were not respectable. After explaining how such role models gave them a preference for immediate gratification, we then have them consider whether they were well-served by such role models.

We look at gangsters who appeared to have reached the pinnacle of the lifestyle and take a closer look at where they are today. We show a videotape featuring two well-known high rollers who tell their own life stories. Their lifestyles were influenced by other negative role models; then, they became such role models themselves. But after a few years of high living, they were targets of police operations. They were indicted, convicted of various federal crimes, and are now in prison for twenty years. Their short-lived high life was a short-term experience, which amounted to nothing more than the early chapters of an empty tragedy.

By seeing what happened to those who attracted them to gang lifestyles, the young men can see that the role models of their youth eventually were failures. They have nothing to show for their charisma, work, and endurance. By helping our young men see how deceptive their role models' trappings of wealth really were and by helping them see how such images influenced them to join gangs, and how their decision ultimately led to their own incarceration, we get them to think about the kinds of images they want to project to other young people when they get out.

We talk about the kind of person these guys could have been if they had been exposed to positive role models and had used their talents and passions constructively. We acknowledge that many of the young men have not been exposed to and influenced by positive models, and we talk about how to make up for that. We focus on what an appropriate role model is and why the others are not appropriate. We demonstrate what eventually happens in the lives of the negative role models.

We have them ask themselves if they are being good role models for youngsters who are trying to decide which way to go in life. We have them recall how young they were when they first became involved in a gang. We have them recall seeing some high roller selling drugs and getting that fast money, and have them consider that they now are playing that role. "Are you helping these little kids see crime as their only option in terms of acquiring material things and gaining status?"

Session Five: Peer Pressure, True Friends, and Independent Thinking

In this session we focus on:

- Resisting negative peer pressure

- Defining true friends

- Discussing the importance of thinking for yourself

It is critical that gang-involved youths learn how to overcome peer pressure. Without the ability to stand up to their former associates, they have no chance of turning around their lives. This is not an easy message for our participants to hear. To them, other gangsters were their family. They went through tough times together and were willing to die for each other. They have a strong bond. Yet, going beyond this bond and turning away from friends in gangs is an absolute necessity if they are to break the cycle of incarceration and violence.

We acknowledge that when they get back into the community, friends and family will welcome them with open arms. They will be excited to see the "fellas," they will want to party and celebrate. Yet, we explain that there is nothing more self-destructive they can do than "kick it" with the "homies."

We tell them knowledge will do them no good unless they apply it. To help them see what is in store, we role-play. One young man will be the person released and other young men will play the former gang members with whom he associated. We let them try to lure him back into his old habits. They offer him drugs and beer, tell him to relax. "We only want to celebrate." They try to stir up his loyalties and offer him some quick money. We have the youth playing the person just released resist them, explaining in a friendly, but firm tone that he has made changes in his life. We suggest things he can say, for instance, he has to meet his parole officer or has to get ready for a job interview. We let the youths playing the "homies" laugh at him for his ambitions and try to wear him down. We show how hard it is going to be to resist the old lifestyle, but we remind him what will happen if he is not strong, if he does not persevere.

As a group, we critique the role-playing and ask what he could have done differently. We find out what was the hardest part of saying "no" to former friends and work on strategies that address that.

We try to arrange a visit with Michael Hall, one of our young men who has been out of the system for almost eight years. We tell them that he was in our program when it just began. So was his best friend. They went through it together and both made good progress.

Michael was so committed to the program that he agreed to stay in the MacLaren Youth Correctional Facility for three extra months to be eligible to participate in a vocational program offered by Willamette Industries. His friends told him he was crazy to stay locked up when he could go home, but he "hung tough." Once he was released, he got a job with Williamette Industries. He saw his prior friends, but always had a good response ready when they wanted him to hang out with them. He was friendly, but was strong enough to say "no" to his former lifestyle.

He kept a low profile, did well at work, and his self-esteem grew. He bought a car and got his own place to live. He gained full independence. Because he had a good work reference, showing that he came to work on time and worked hard, Nike hired him. He has been working for the company for more than five years. He has been promoted more than once and is so well liked and appreciated by his co-workers that they raised money to send him to his mother's funeral, which was in another state.

His friend, on the other hand, a young man who had the same opportunities as Michael, could not resist his old friends. He went out on a few interviews, got frustrated, and eventually went back into his old lifestyle. His goals faded away, and he was charged with attempted murder. He is serving ten- to twelve-years in an adult prison.

We let the young men know we will do everything in our power to help them, but ultimately, it is going to be up to them to have the strength to make the right decisions. We can give them the tools, but they will have to construct the bridge to a new life. Old friends, no matter how deep the relationship, will impede their progress if they ask them to go back to their old ways. We explain that they have to know the difference between friend and foe. A friend would not ask them to die for them. A friend would congratulate them on their efforts to make something out of themselves, to get out of the mix. A friend would not want them to be ignorant. A friend would be impressed with their efforts to further their education. A friend would not want them to risk going back to prison for selling drugs. A friend would celebrate with them when they got a real job. A friend would not hinder their goals. Instead, a friend would do everything he or she could to help them attain their dreams.

We say "There are friends like we're describing, ones who want the best for you. Find them and stick with them. Leave the others behind." We encourage them to share their knowledge with others who still may be in the gangs if they think they are receptive to it.

And we remind them over and over and over again, there is no "half-stepping it." There is no hanging out with the boys on a part-time basis. Their commitment has to be total or their work in this program will be wasted, and they will have greater problems in the future.

Removing Self-imposed Booby Traps

Sometimes young men about to return to the community will express strong doubts about their ability to stay away from gangs, drugs, and crime because of the environment they will be in, which will include rivals, enemies, opportunities to buy and sell drugs, and other negative factors. Although the risks always will be there, we remind them that there is a lot they can do to avoid them or minimize their impact.

One way is to consistently project a certain image. We tell them the following.

> If you're still wearing clothing that ties you in with the gang culture, such as Dickies with your pants sagging, nobody's going to think you're for real. But if you wear clothes that reflect your new attitude and image that you want to present to the community, your chances of being successful will be increased. If you know of certain hotbeds for criminal and gang activity, stay away from them.
>
> Occupy your time with constructive endeavors. Only associate with positive, optimistic people who have the same desire you have. Stay away from those who are dealing drugs and engaging in gang activity. The way you act and the things you do, say more to the community about your former lifestyle than any words you speak.
>
> When you first get out, law enforcement, for example, will look to see you in your old familiar haunts. If, instead, they see that you are working, going to school, and helping build up the community, they will be more likely to treat you with increased respect and not be so quick to 'sweat you'.

Session Six: Anger Management, Conflict Resolution, and Mediation

In this session we focus on:

- Handling anger, frustration, and conflict in appropriate ways

- Identifying situations that may cause anger

- Finding ways to avoid or defuse volatile situations

A lot of our young men have responded to frustration and anger with physical or verbal violence for most of their lives. We acknowledge that they almost certainly will face some frustration when they return to their communities. There might be family problems and/or money problems. It is unlikely they will get the first job for which they apply. Their old girlfriend might be seeing somebody else and want nothing to do with them. No doubt they will have good reasons to be angry and frustrated, and it is how they handle this situation that will determine their success.

We talk about ways to manage and contain anger. We give them coping skills to help them understand themselves and to learn how to apply various strategies for regaining their composure after being provoked. We teach them the importance of recognizing things that trigger anger and show them how to use strategies for effectively pulling themselves out before they get to the real hurtful state. We do a lot of role-playing with hypothetical, anger-producing situations.

One role-play we do focuses on the frustration of not getting a job quickly. We set up a mock interview, and they get turned down four times. Someone plays one of their "homies" who says, "Told you nobody would want somebody who's been locked up. Come on back with me. I'll set you up."

The so-called friend does indeed set him up. He is hanging out selling drugs, and he gets arrested. He is on parole already. He is going straight back to lock-up.

We do the same role-play, but this time, instead of turning to an old friend, he talks to a positive friend or someone he has worked with who is trying to help him build a new life. This friend says, "I know it is tough, but I have faith in you. You're strong. You can do it." The friend feels the frustration the young man is going through, makes some phone calls, and tells him about some other possibilities. Maybe he introduces him to a community leader who is impressed with his efforts and tries to help him out. We show him that the support to do right is there, but he must go to the right places to find it and that perseverance is essential.

Another role-play we do is one in which a family member is threatened. We tell them this situation very well could happen. They have been locked up for violence. Someone might want revenge.

> When you get out, you might hear that someone's going to go after your mother or brother to get even for the damage you did to their family. Before you go off to 'protect' your loved one, you need to stop and think. Would your mother really want you shooting at someone? Would she be proud that her son was a murderer? Would she be happy that you brought another woman the pain of having her child killed? Would she be proud of you for going back to jail, for continuing your criminal ways? No. She would want you to be strong, to change your ways, to prove that you have learned things and to see that you are committed to a new life. Sure, it would be tough to see a family member hurt or threatened, but it is not an excuse to get back into 'banging,' and if you retaliate, that is just where you will be. Your family wants you safe and productive. If you do regress, do not say you are doing it for somebody else's safety. Be honest and own up to the fact that you are doing it for yourself.

We acknowledge that there will be times when they will be targeted for their past behavior, but we point out that they need to deal with it by taking time out, by talking to a positive person, and by talking to someone who can help diffuse the situation before it gets out of hand. It is not weakness to ask for help; it shows strong character to follow through on the commitment not to revert to old ways, not to participate in the violence destroying the community. We repeatedly tell them, "We never said it'll be easy. It won't be, but if you 'hang tough' and you're strong, you *will* make it."

We stress over and over that to succeed, they cannot let anger or frustration get the best of them. They have to learn how to keep those feelings from escalating. Self-control is essential to succeed in society. The hope is that they will apply the information we have shared with them when they need it most. "Your ability to control your anger will dictate if you will be successful." We also tell them

72

they could get a job, and then be passed over for promotion and get negative about this situation. We want to give them more appropriate ways to respond to such frustrations. Additionally, we provide them with tools for mediating conflict between others. Peacemaking is a skill which provides growth for all involved. As with other subjects, we have former gang members and others from the community come in to talk about how they achieved personal or professional success by maintaining control of their anger in the face of provocation.

Session Seven: Self-knowledge Through Historical Awareness

In this session we focus on:

- Learning about people of color who have made a difference in the world

- Understanding the contributions of minority cultures to society

- Recognizing minority traditions and celebrations

Many young men do not have a knowledge of their history, either within their families or as a race. They do not know where they come from. They have no sense of the sacrifices that their race made to get where they are in this country. Consequently, they are unaware of their pivotal connection to their future as a race and as a nation.

We have found that participants' willingness to reexamine their values is best achieved when they are able to view their lives as a meaningful part of an ongoing history of a people. We include African-American history in our curriculum for African-American youth to give them a stronger sense of who they are.

We talk about their ancestors who were captured, bound in chains, and brought to this country in the hulls of ships to be slaves. If they had believed that they never could be more than slaves as readily as so many are willing to accept the notion that they must be in gangs, we still might be enslaved today. But because they saw themselves as children of God and were willing to fight and sacrifice for their freedom, we have our freedom today. "Our ancestors dealt with many atrocities during the times of slavery and the subsequent Jim Crow laws." We spend time getting our young men to understand that "we are a strong and proud race that has overcome insurmountable odds to achieve greatness in the face of oppression. We have given much to this nation."

When we begin this session, we ask our young men if they are proud of their race or culture. Most raise their hands. We say, "Knock those hands down. Here you are selling drugs, being violent, committing genocide, being problems in your community."

We show them how they can help their communities and their culture by being positive. This, in turn, builds self-esteem and helps them. They start to discover who they are inside by being connected to a larger picture.

We ask them, "What are your goals? Your ambitions? What do you love? What moves you inside?" Many times they never have been asked to think about these things. They never had to put it into words. When they begin to look for these answers, they begin to discover who they are.

> You are not the labels that have been put on you — labels that your gang gave you, that your teachers gave you when you caused trouble, that society gives you because you have committed crimes. You are a human being just like everyone else, and you have the power to make your life count for something good. Be proud of your heritage. Be proud of who you are inside.

Session Eight: Racism and Prejudice

In this session we focus on:

- Honoring cultural diversity in people

- Not allowing prejudice and racism to gain control of their lives

- Finding appropriate methods for dealing with racism and prejudice

- Engaging in self-examination of attitudes towards other races, cultures, and women

This session is an extension of the social skills that come with self-growth. The ability to relate to a broad range of people should be one of the qualities of a maturing person because successful people in our country respect differences in people and do not allow differences to keep them from accomplishing things of value to the society. We spend considerable time discussing how each one of us is different from each other and how, conversely, each of us has many things in common.

For young people who at one point were willing to take another's life based on such things as gang colors or handsigns, it can be quite a challenge to get them to change gears and look only for things they have in common with people from very different backgrounds, lifestyles, and ethnicities. Getting them to do this helps them understand how difficult it must be for others to accept them and to give them trust and respect because of their criminal records, their gang markings, and possibly even their race. The irony of having that in common with people they had automatically labeled as racist, biased, and unfair often can be quite unsettling.

We share other potential problem areas with them. For instance, many of them have their own prejudices towards white people. They blame white people and racism for many of our problems today. We show them that "we no longer can use racism as an excuse for what we are doing to each other. We must be able to educate ourselves."

We tell them, "You cannot let racism get power over you. Do not give racism more credit than it deserves. Very little can stop an educated African-American man who knows who he is, where he came from, and where he wants to go. Such a man, with a strong desire to benefit his people, his family and his community, is a powerful man."

We do not deny racism exists, but we point out that we have been dealing with it in this country for 200 years, and we have made a lot of progress despite it. We also point out that many white people are not racists. We help our young men develop the ability to relate to people of various races and cultures, and we teach them how to maintain self-control when racism does present itself.

Without the ability to get along with diverse groups of people, there is little chance of doing well in a country that is becoming increasingly diverse. We point this out and stress the importance of respecting people different than they are. We show them that they can grow and gain knowledge by accepting other people and their cultures. We ask them to deal with their own prejudices — to look at the individual and not the race.

One role play we do demonstrates the importance of not letting racial tensions interfere with a job. A young man plays the part of an employee who is doing well in a customer service job. He gets to work on time, has learned new skills, and gets along with people. Just when there is a possibility of a promotion, another young man comes in to the company and makes a racist remark. The original employee ignores him. The new employee calls him more names.

Then, the original employee gets mad, reacts, and security is called. The manager is informed about what happened. The manager understands that the original employee was insulted, but now he is not going to give him a promotion. The manager is trying to run a business and cannot have an employee who cannot handle pressure while on the job.

We recreate the scene, but this time, the youth is asked to refrain from anger. He does his best to help a customer without getting into an argument. The boss sees it and when the customer leaves, his boss tells him how impressed he is with the way he handled himself. He has proven to his boss that he can keep cool under fire. He has shown some strength. We also point out that in this or similar situations, he could have excused himself and asked someone else to take over for him. Doing so would not show weakness, but rather good judgment.

What we tell them is simple: "racism is not an excuse. You are strong. You can deal with it."

Session Nine: Values Clarification

In this session we focus on:

- Identifying negative values that led to criminal or gang activity

- Discovering how we learn and pass on values

- Providing a humorous look at cultural values throughout history

- Defining appropriate values

Gangsters' values are contrary to social norms. We have the young men examine the values that underlie gang activity. They compare those mores with those of the larger society. We have them explain how and why the values differ and why society rejects the values underlying criminal behavior. We talk about the kind of values one needs to be successful in this society. We discuss moral values, responsibility, and honesty. Essentially, we talk about what it takes to be considered a good person.

We ask, "To be successful in this society, what values must you have?" We talk a lot about changing values and behaviors, but in this exercise, we get specific. We look at the thinking errors that are associated with criminal behavior and have them consider why society regards criminals negatively. We have the participants come up with better ways of thinking. We help them develop a positive value base by identifying the values necessary to be successful in a conventional way. We ask questions and let the truth come from them, because then they understand it far better than if they were simply told.

We try to replace negative gang values with positive values that will help the youth succeed. Negative gang values include the desire for immediate gratification (in other words, getting quick money by selling drugs and robbing people), being dishonest, manipulating, being violent (such as engaging in drive-by shootings or assaults), being hostile or displaying an uncaring attitude toward others (including those not in their "set" and females), and interacting with others (such as by using "put-downs," fighting, and challenging others).

The positive values we stress include displaying patience (versus seeking immediate gratification), taking responsibility, showing respect for others, honoring diversity, being honest and behaving with integrity, honoring commitments, working hard, appreciating the value of education, and engaging in nonviolent conflict resolution.

Session Ten: Individual Responsibility, Self-determination and Goal Setting

In this session we focus on:

- Taking individual responsibility for life

- Putting forth the commitment and determination necessary to achieve goals

- Setting long- and short-range goals

- Evaluating realistic versus unrealistic goals

- Overcoming obstacles

- Reaching goals one small step at a time

A lot of guys have excuses for their criminal behavior and gang involvement. They blame their families, the system, lack of job opportunities, the white man, the power structure — the list is end-less. We put the responsibility squarely on them.

As staff, we are sensitive and understand the many obstacles they face in life and the cumulative impact of them. We recognize that their life has not been fair in many ways, but we let them know that they, themselves, are the ones most likely to make their life successful. We confidently tell them that they must take indi-vidual responsibility for their lives.

We say, "Just because you come from a bad situation does not mean that you have to be a bad person." We remind them that there are many examples of people who have overcome adversity in their lives and have become successful, productive people. We show them they cannot continue to blame others for the fact that they are acting out and being negative.

We tell them that while it is important to visualize the kind of image they want to project, it is of utmost importance to know themselves truly — who they are as individuals. They must know and love themselves. We look at self-esteem and help them identify areas of esteem in themselves.

We look at failures that result from avoiding individual respon-sibility. We also talk about the cause-and-effect relationship between insecurity about their individual responsibility. A person who is secure in himself has less difficulty owning up to his actions and accepting praise or blame for them. On the other hand, a per-son who is not sure of himself or the image he is projecting, but knows only that he probably is not viewed positively, will be less willing to accept responsibility for his actions and their results.

One important issue we talk about is the need to grow continu-ally as an individual. Gang involvement arrests personal growth and keeps one locked at a low level of motivation to keep in sync with the "homeboys." We emphasize that the "homeboys" will feel uncomfortable when these young men start thinking and acting for themselves. Unlike the "homies," we want the participants to grow and open up their minds to new experiences.

We will not accept the notion that our young people have to be in gangs if they grow up in a particular environment. Nor do we accept the notion that once in a gang, one cannot get out and suc-cessfully stay out. We understand the factors that contribute to belonging to gangs, and we acknowledge their feelings, but we work with them to liberate their self-expectation.

A lot of guys think only of the moment. We help our participants see that they must prepare today for the future. This may include education and training to develop marketable skills. We help them set short- and long-term goals and strategies to pursue their goals. We demonstrate that they must make plans for themselves to make progress in life. We want them to understand that a lot of people never make it because they are unable to follow through on their goals. It is not always a smooth ride. But we tell them in this session and in the sessions on conflict resolution, that it is up to them to avoid being distracted by the obstacles. They must jump over hurdles to achieve their goals.

Session Eleven: Maximum Benefits from a Minimum-wage Job

In this session we focus on:

- Exploding the myths of minimum-wage jobs as a deadend

- Working for the things they want

- Building on work experience to forge a career path

As mentioned earlier, we have a generation of young people who seem to believe they should not have to work hard to be successful, that it is better to rob people and sell drugs to get things quickly. A common refrain among many young people today is that "I ain't workin' no burger flippin' minimum wage job at Mickie D's." The message we want to implant is that they can have material things and be successful, but they have to work hard and grow as an individual. Again, the tone for such discussions is not lecturing, "you better take jobs like this because you really cannot do any better." Instead, we have them take a sober look at the reasons for such negative attitudes about this kind of work and the people who perform it, and also look at what these positions have to offer someone.

They have been conditioned to believe that all life holds for them is a minimum-wage job. They reason that if all the marketplace has to offer in the way of legitimate work is a minimum wage and life at the poverty level, they might as well sell drugs and live large for as long as the pleasure lasts, however short and dangerous the experience might be.

We seek to destroy the myth that if you start at minimum wage, you always will be paid a minimum wage. We show these young men that most people with successful lives today started out at "square one." We provide many examples of how a job can turn into a career, which can turn into a future. We tell them "there is nothing wrong about working for minimum wage when you're a teenager. An entry-level job is just that — an entry into the work-place. It is unreasonable to expect an executive's pay when they are just starting out.

We educate them about the benefits of accepting a minimum-wage job to develop a track record to show they are responsible. Entry-level jobs prove they can handle working in the workforce and provide an opportunity to learn the effort it takes to get up in the morning to be at work on time. We tell them:

> Working in a restaurant will teach you valuable skills, such as how to be a team member, how to work the cash register, how to do bookkeeping. Mainly, you learn what the labor market is about, and you'll be able to make realistic assessments of your goals and abilities. Experience allows you to get references, to set foundations on which to build. When you see an opportunity to move up and make more money, you'll be able to come in with a reference if you do well on your first job.

We bring in people who came from very poor backgrounds, who started out in a minimum-wage position, set short- and long-term goals for themselves, persevered, and are successful today. We hear about the goals they set, the strategies they pursued, and the setbacks they overcame along the way to get where they are. Because success may be in the eye of the beholder, such guests may include anyone from the head of a corporate business to a mother of five children raising them all to be responsible adults while putting herself through school.

It would not be realistic or consistent to expect instant conversions to this work ethic or for youths, who have been conditioned to prefer fast money, to set goals. After all, if we preach patience and realistic goal-setting, we must model these qualities in our work with them.

We are fortunate to have the continued support of three young men who completed our program. They have retained interest in our program and regularly come and share their experiences with other young men. They demonstrate that it is possible to get out of a gang lifestyle and to become productive.

These young men, Ronnie, Mike, and James, usually are well received as they explain how, after completing our program, they were patient enough to take minimum-wage, entry-level positions with a regional restaurant chain. They tell how they gradually are advancing up the ladder, one rung at a time. They tell of getting more responsibilities and the pay that comes with it. They give us progress reports of how they are establishing better lives and long-term security for their families and themselves. These young men say:

> I'm working. I'm handling things differently. I know what you're going to face, and I'm telling you it can be done because I did it. Forget the myth that once you're in a gang you cannot get out.

It is ultimately gratifying to see youths absorbing and applying the principles we stress. And it is even more gratifying that acting on these principals produces the kinds of results we have seen in the trio of graduates who have been so generous with their time and encouragement.

Session Twelve: Personal Growth as a Lifelong Mission

In this session we focus on:

- Understanding the doors that a good education opens

- Appreciating the importance of technical skills

- Seeing the direct correlation between education, training, and good jobs

- Examing educational opportunities

- Locating apprenticeship programs

We are good at helping youth see the need to get out of gangs and make the commitment, but the work is not done yet. In fact, it only has begun. We must broaden and personalize the focus by helping each young man see his own personal growth as his highest priority for the next few years. We must help each one believe, as we do, that all that he does, thinks, and believes for the remainder of his time in juvenile corrections, and everything he does, thinks, and believes from the day he is released, is all part of a process of personal growth that will continue for the rest of his life.

Part of this growth process includes reassessing the value of education. Coming into the program, many of these young men have disliked school and education, in general. We help them see how many more options they can have with a high school diploma, and how much more likely they are to be successful if they can go on to college. An education can help them regain control of their lives. We point out that what we have been doing in our sessions is, in fact, education. They need to regard the subjects covered in school — such as math, grammar, science, and history — as highly as the subjects we cover in our sessions, because they, too, have practical application in their lives and in the job market.

Session Thirteen: Job Opportunities and Entrepreneurship

In this session we focus on:

- Considering available jobs
- Looking at the current job market
- Getting an overview of the business community
- Understanding what it takes to be an entrepreneur
- Learning how to find a job that is right for them
- Training for the job they want

We use this time to talk about potential job opportunities and the process of looking for work. We work through a job-readiness curriculum that includes finding a job, interviewing, and holding onto a job, and communicating effectively with coworkers and supervisors.

Our discussions includes a look at entrepreneurship. We tell them they should not rule out lawful self-employment. Not only do we suggest that they can run their own businesses, but we also introduce them to people and organizations who can help them start and run such a businesses. We also talk about the complications and pitfalls that persons with inadequate education, training, and resources experience when going into business for themselves. The discussions of self-employment are valuable, even if they do not result in anyone going into business for himself, because, among other things, we have them view work from an employer's perspective.

By asking, "What kind of person do I want to employ in my business?" we have them consider the kind of person they ought to be if they want someone else to hire them. This is important to do before they have any job interviews.

Leadership

In this session, we talk about the qualities of a positive leader. We focus on thinking for yourself and feeling good about yourself. We ask them the qualities a leader has and have them create lists. Attributes we include on the list include the following:

- Being able to think for themselves
- Having the strength to stand up for what is right
- Acting with integrity and honor
- Having perseverance in the face of adversity
- Helping others, caring about their families and communities
- Setting a good example

We stress that the first person that they must be able to lead is themselves. Thus, self-knowledge is important. We have dialogs about the attributes of great leaders. This empowers the participants to be strong and committed to their own self-determination.

Session Fourteen: Child Rearing

In this session we focus on:

- Appreciating the importance of a father in a child's life
- Knowing what being a good parent means
- Learning how to meet a child's physical and emotional needs

Unfortunately, at any given time, a significant percentage of our students are fathers. Others become fathers while in the institution. We spend time teaching what being a responsible parent entails. We acknowledge that biologically almost anyone can bring a life into this world, but it takes a real man to care for, love, and provide for his children.

The importance of this subject cannot be overstated. If not already parents, many of our participants will be in the near future. By engaging our young men in discussions about the physical and emotional needs of children in their various stages of development, we start them thinking about the kind of role models they must be for their children. In our sessions, our young men identify key persons and events that affected their development both positively and negatively. As they trace their steps and missteps, they are able to express with surprising clarity and insight, the things they will need to include and/or eliminate from their lives and the lives of their children for the children to mature into caring, responsible adults.

We Must Model Patience

The emphasis in this work is that you should not try to "preach" to the youths with whom you work. This alienates them, and they may use your stance to justify their gangster lifestyle as opposed to the "square" lifestyles you seem to be offering as an alternative.

Yet, in fact, we do lay down some high octane sermons, but only when the circumstances are right. As with any conversion process, there is a time when a sermon that "hits between the eyes" is entirely appropriate. We have learned that the first few sessions are not the time for a sermon. Only after you have a well-established, trusting relationship with the youths in your program can you proceed with the type of frank talk outlined in this chapter.

If you head off to a group discussion armed with the magic beans of this chapter without having taken the time to till and soften the soil, and lay the appropriate foundation, your stalk will not grow, and you may find more frustration than you ever had imagined possible.

A high degree of commitment is necessary to create, implement, and sustain a gang-intervention program. No one should operate out of a misconception that after reading this book, unbounded success will be just around the corner.

A friend of the author slimmed down to his high school weight of 229 pounds after weighing more than 300 pounds. He has exceeded his weight-loss goal in dramatic fashion. If you ask him how he did it, he is almost at a loss for an explanation. He had set 240 pounds as his goal and made so many changes in his lifestyle to reach it over the past four years, that they gradually became ingrained into his daily routine. Now, he can hardly remember the things he eliminated, changed, or worked into his daily routine to achieve success.

Similarly, it is easy to forget some of the very real frustration and pain we had to deal with as we were getting this program off the ground. One might think that gaining the full support of the administration would be the most difficult challenge in the process. Not so. Instead, the greatest obstacle, and the reason we nearly abandoned our effort, came from the very people we wanted to help.

The young men already had given up on themselves and believed that society already had given up on them. They figured that it would just be a matter of time before we, too, would deem them unworthy of a long-term effort and stopped being committed to their personal growth and success.

The author has experienced profound frustration working with this population. He almost gave up on the program. He thought he was a good facilitator. He had a background similar to the kids in the program as well as professional program treatment experience. Plus, he had a degree in social work and certainly understood the sociological perspectives. But the first six months were really tough. "Even though we had a relationship with the young men and they were in the program voluntarily, they challenged us at every possible opportunity. They did not readily accept our views. They still clung to their gangster mentality."

The author left one session downright angry with the youth, ready to forget about them altogether. Who needed the grief and aggravation? He was doing everything he could to help them. People had backed them when nobody wanted to hear one more word about gang kids, and instead of hearing what we were saying, realizing we were trying to give them a chance in life, they were not particularly receptive to our ideas. What was the point?

But then, the author stopped himself. These kids were real good at getting people to believe they could not change. They had alienated family members with their defiance. They had gotten kicked out of school. They were defiant to law officials and had been arrested. They were masters at getting people to give up on them. They wanted the author to give up on them. That would further justify their lifestyle. The author had to do some serious soul searching to stay committed. But if he did not believe they could change, why should they? He had to persevere just like he was asking them to do, even though they were not responding on his time line. He took a deep breath, calmed down, and went back to work — work that has paid off again and again.

This narration emphasizes the degree of commitment you need before you ever start to design a gang-intervention strategy. You must anticipate and have genuine responses, not pat answers. And, you must be willing, like we ask our participants to be, to endure the trying times.

You will know that your program is becoming more effective when you see evidence of a positive culture in the program, or positive leadership among your youth. In working with this population, there is no more satisfying achievement to be realized. It is a struggle to get there, and you can expect that there will be times when you are ready to admit defeat, but your perseverance will be rewarded.

7

the need for enhanced programs

There is no one solution to ending gang involvement, nor is there one person who has the full array of answers. However, this chapter presents some of the minimum elements of a successful transition strategy for youths completing the kind of gang-intervention program that has been successful at the MacLaren Youth Correctional Facility.

Making Time Serve Us

We cannot always control how long we have the young men in our institutions. While we must try to make as much steady progress as we can with each young man we serve, the metamorphosis from gang-banger to stable, self-sufficient, civic-minded adult may take years.

Considering all the work and services each gang-involved youth requires to achieve permanent reformation, our efforts may amount to little more than planting a seed that must be watered, protected, and harvested years after their release from incarceration.

Opportunities for Service

We use several programs to give our young men opportunities to be constructive forces, both within and beyond our walls.

Cultural Awareness Assemblies

On campus, we offer our young men the opportunity to plan and perform programs before the entire campus. Programs include assemblies for Black History Month, Cinco de Mayo, graduations, and other uplifting occasions.

These programs offer an extraordinary opportunity for the youths to participate in an event that allows them to demonstrate their abilities — abilities they might not even be aware that they have. This showcases the talents and creativity of the young men, often for the first time.

We have held the Black History Month assembly since 1988. Each year, the assembly becomes bigger and stronger. Originally, we began this assembly to celebrate the African-American youths' cultural heritage. The participants were required to research the lives of African Americans who had contributed to the growth and development of our country. Many learned the history of their culture for the first time. As they began to learn about their cultural heritage, they began to have pride in who they were and where they came from. They saw that they were connected to something far bigger than their "set" or gang. They saw how hard their ancestors worked to accomplish goals, and little by little, their loyalty to their gang lifestyle gave way to a desire to be part of something bigger — to participate in bettering the lives of those around them instead of hurting the communities their ancestors fought so hard to build.

Since they were to perform before the entire campus, they worked hard to create something in which they could shine. They wrote songs, poetry, raps, and speeches that expressed pride in their history and in themselves. Most of our young men had never had a chance to perform in front of an audience. Some were nervous, but as we worked together as a group, supporting every individual's effort, they began to believe in themselves, to know that they could do something positive. Their efforts are rewarded year after year with standing ovations, and staff members frequently begin to see the participants in a new light — to respect the gifts they have. There is no way to measure the impact this kind of recognition has on our youths.

The First Black History Assembly

The first assembly is worth its own section because it demonstrated that we were on the right track. This assembly surpassed our expectations. Rival gang members put aside their rivalries and worked together to present a program celebrating their common heritage. Side by side, they learned about their history and created a program celebrating the accomplishments of African Americans.

This was the first time most of our participants had worked on a long-term goal. They learned that success does not happen overnight. They worked and reworked their speeches and presentations until they were ready to perform in front of a standing-room only crowd. They saw that with effort, they could do things they had never thought possible, and they realized that with work, they could accomplish their goals. As the day for the assembly approached, we were ecstatic. A dream was about to be fulfilled. But then, tragedy struck.

The day before the assembly, a well-known Crip member was murdered in Portland. Most of our participants knew him. We were horrified that all the work our youths had done together might be undone, that gang rivalries might erupt, and that loyalties could undermine all of our efforts with these young men. Instead, the youths rallied round and proved to us that our efforts had not been in vain. Despite the obvious pain the youths who had personally known the victim felt, they wanted the assembly to go on as scheduled. They told us that this tragic death added greater meaning to their show.

The former Bloods in our group felt the loss their former rivals were feeling. They expressed empathy and concern. There was no gloating, no victory.

When these young men took the stage despite their sorrow, we saw the support former rivals offered each other, when they performed together, celebrating their heritage, we knew everything we had done to that point — the frustrations and doubts, the sleepless nights and self-examinations — had been worth it. These youths, former perpetrators of violence and criminal acts, were worth every moment of our efforts.

You, too, will see your efforts rewarded. There will be setbacks, there will be doubts, but there will also be shining moments when you know that you have succeeded in giving those young people who many others thought beyond hope a chance to grow and to accomplish if not great, then surely significant things.

Benefits of the Assembly

The assembly provided a chance for others in the community to meet the youths and work with them. Dancers, teachers, and performers help the youth prepare. These volunteers do not treat the kids as failures, as so many adults often have done in the past, but as talented, gifted performers who have things to share and show others. Our youths respond to this support, and there is no trace of hardened gangsters when they step up onto the stage.

It takes nearly two months to prepare for the assembly, and the participants become stronger and more dedicated every day. We invite community leaders and politicians to the assembly. We invite and honor alumni who have been out for several years and are making progress with their lives. Church groups come to sing hymns.

The assembly not only demonstrates to the community that we have not given up on the kids, but it also proves to the youths that they have begun to discover their talents and strengths. It proves to them in a very concrete way that what they have to offer is appreciated and will be recognized postively. They begin to realize that effort and hard work has rewards.

The Cinco de Mayo celebration has the same effect on the Hispanic students. We see the same cultural pride develop, and the same connection to their history grows. We witness a subtle transformation in the youths as they celebrate their heritage and their own abilities. Often, for the first time in their lives, they feel connected to something important, and they see that they can receive attention for being positive, that they do not have to be tough or carry a gun to earn respect.

For our 1997 cultural awareness assemblies, our auditorium had standing-room only. State Senator Avel Gordley, the first African-American-woman in this position spoke, encouraging our youth to continue demonstrating that they can turn their lives around. Having a person as important as a state senator show support for them had a profound impact on the youth. Hearing that she believed in them and hearing her urge the community to help these youths lead productive lives was a stirring message.

While our African-American assemblies focus on the African-American culture, our programs are ethnically diverse and everyone, regardless of race, has an opportunity to participate in the assembly. Hispanic, Asian, Native American, and Caucasian youth all have been involved in these assemblies. In addition to helping the youths in our program in a number of ways, cultural celebrations also bring staff and youth together in valuing diversity.

Positive Peer Groups

Positive peer groups have grown out of the Minority Youth Concerns Program on the MacLaren Youth Correctional Facility campus. The first one developed about six months into the program when some of the participants approached us and told us that they were committed to reclaiming their lives. They asked for a program that would give them more than the orientation. They wanted to learn more skills, to help others, in turn. It was an incredibly rewarding moment and made all the frustration we had experienced worth it.

This first positive peer group was called Brothers Chillin' Positive (BCP). Staff worked with the members on issues in greater depth than we had before. They were eager to learn, eager to try out more skills, and it was a pleasure to work with them. They supported each other and helped newcomers who had not earned any special privileges. They wrote speeches about what young people needed to do to make a better world and tried to help others understand the dangers of violence.

We taught the BCP's participants how to resolve conflicts and how to help others on campus to do that, as well. They helped minimize gang influence and racial tension in the institution.

To be part of BCP, students had to actively participate in the minority program and had to demonstrate consistent progress in changing their negative gang lifestyle. The members focused intensely on education, vocational skill-training, and job opportunities as they worked to become positive role models and find ways to give something back to the community.

Other positive peer groups have emerged over the years, all with similar missions. Our staff plays no leadership role in these groups other than to schedule the meetings and provide staff presence for security purposes. We have had full support from the administration for all of these groups.

In their meetings, the young men reinforce each other's commitment to leave gang-banging behind and talk about how to deal with the various obstacles and temptations awaiting them in the community.

To participate in the positive peer group, youths must:

- Actively participate in the minority youth concerns program

- Disassociate themselves from gang behaviors, attitudes, and image

- Project positive behaviors, attitudes, and images on campus

- Demonstrate positive leadership on campus

- Successfully participate in other programs on campus, such as drug and alcohol, sex offender, reality therapy, violent offender, and so forth

- Assist in maintaining peace between students when racial gang, or ethnic tensions develop, when they are called upon to do so

- Work on achieving a high-school diploma or GED

- Commit themselves to self-growth and to become a productive member of the community

We provide positive peer group members the opportunity to go off-campus and take trips to the Oregon coast, parks, or go on dinner outings. These activities expose them, often for the first time, to beautiful, positive settings. They also provide an opportunity for the young men to see us and each other as people, like themselves, with common likes and dislikes, with a positive view of the future. It is sadly true that many of these young men had to be incarcerated for serious offenses before experiencing the kind of outings and uplifting experiences we in the past expected families, youth programs, and schools to provide.

Community Service Efforts

Community outreach is a major component of this group's activities. Participants in this program go to schools, professional organizations, the Oregon legislature, churches, youth service providers, and other groups to educate people on the dangers of gangs, drugs, and violence, and the value of programs such as ours.

We "R" One

Marion Wright Edelman, director of the Children's Defense Fund, states in an article on gangs:

Never before has our country seen, or permitted the epidemic of gangs and violence that is turning our communities into fearful, armed camps and sapping the lives and hopes of so many of our children. Never have we seen such a dangerous, domestic arms race. Never has America permitted children to rely on guns and gangs, rather than parents and neighbors, for protection and love, or pushed so many into the tumultuous sea of life without the lifevest of nurturing families and communities, challenged minds, job prospects and hope. This is not the dream that Dr. Martin Luther King, Jr. spoke of thirty years ago. This is a modern nightmare that must end!

The influence and attraction to gangs for many youth often begins at a very young age. It is therefore critical that gang-prevention efforts and strategies be implemented at the earliest possible grade school levels, to begin working on initiating the type of self-esteem and awareness necessary to help youths resist the lure of gangs. Lincoln Elementary School and the MacLaren Youth Correctional Facility Minority Concerns Program formed such a partnership. We developed an innovative gang-prevention program to help youths resist the temptation of gangs while promoting the positive self-growth of youths. This program grew out of one of our positive peer groups.

Called "We 'R' One," this positive peer-group community outreach program is an innovative antigang, antidrug, and antiviolence curriculum that positive peer group participants codeveloped and facilitated at Lincoln Elementary School in Woodburn, Oregon in 1994.

Lincoln Elementary School is located about three miles from the MacLaren Youth Correctional Facility. The population includes a significant number of students who have family members active in gangs. Lead counselor Nancy Merzenich thought that perhaps an assembly with gang members who had been incarcerated for crimes and who had come to see the negative impact of a gang lifestyle would help steer impressionable young students away from gangs.

The assembly was so successful that Nancy Merzenich, our staff, and the positive peer group designed a program that targeted all 600 students at Lincoln. The objective of the program was to help deromanticize gangs in the minds of young kids.

Not everyone at the elementary school liked the idea. Some staff were worried that it would increase, rather than decrease, the students' desire to join a gang. Some families were unhappy that incarcerated juveniles would come to their school and be around their young children. They did not want their children to hear about drugs, gangs, and violence. So, we called a meeting and invited all concerned adults, including parents, to come to talk about our program. It was extremely disheartening that so few people attended.

We had many sessions with our positive peer group. We explained that we were making a long-term commitment — an entire year — and that they needed to meet the challenge. They would have to come prepared. They would need a program that would keep the young students interested and involved. They had to be ready to answer tough questions. They would need to be involved in the classroom and in recreational activities.

The program got off to a good start, despite the lack of interest shown at the meeting we called. Some staff were still apprehensive, some parents still disgruntled, and some people waited for us to fail. But we dug in, knowing we could succeed.

Our students served as facilitators for sessions conducted in various classrooms over three hours. Among the subjects we covered in our weekly We 'R' One visits to Lincoln were the following:

- Exploring the negatives of gang membership

- Setting educational and other goals

- Learning value clarification

- Building leadership and self-esteem

- Understanding peer pressure and defining true friends

- Honoring cultural diversity

- Using conflict resolution

- Resisting drugs and alcohol

In addition to classroom sessions on violence, drugs, and gangs, our peer group also spent time with students during recreation periods, interacting and developing positive relationships with the young students.

At the end of the first year, we held an end-of-the year celebration. Unlike the meeting at the beginning of the program, this was well attended — over 600 people came. We had T-shirts for all the kids, and the peer group members were honored with plaques from the classroom teachers. Oregon Supreme Court Justice Robert Durham and the Executive Director of the State Commission on Children and Families, Diane Walton, were the guest speakers.

A letter written by Nancy Merzenich best demonstrates the success of the program:

> Five to twelve years old . . . each student at Lincoln Elementary in Woodburn, Oregon, sat in awe as three MacLaren Youth Correctional Facility inmates shared their stories . . . stories about the gang lifestyle that led them to getting locked up. Natasha was up on her knees, hand in the air, questions on her lips and eyes open wide with wonder. Jose couldn't sit still. His own experiences related too much to what these MacLaren Youth Correctional Facility youths had lived and he couldn't wait to talk about what his life was like with his gangster father and uncles and aunts.
>
> I watched the magic that was occurring in the lives of these gang-prone (and not so gang-prone) youngsters and the self-esteem that was growing before my eyes in these MacLaren Youth Correctional Facility youth and knew that there was power in this combination. The staff from MacLaren Youth Correctional Facility, under the guidance of Lonnie Jackson, experienced that precious moment and also caught the vision.
>
> Lonnie, his staff and I got together and brainstormed what we thought could happen in our quest for gang prevention and intervention. Before the next school year began, we had our We 'R' One purpose, curriculum, schedule, and kick-off assembly planned. Of course, it wasn't all easy street. Teachers and parents questioned MacLaren Youth Correctional Facility inmates coming into their classroom. 'Will these guys glorify gangs? Will my kids be safe?' Could this backfire and encourage rather than discourage gang involvement? With the support of the administration, the trust of staff and parents, and an evening meeting with everyone involved to discuss the venture, We 'R' One got off the ground.
>
> The guys were ready each week for their 15-20 minute classroom presentations from the curriculum that had been

devised. Their role-plays and passionate pleas for healthy lifestyle choices won the hearts of teachers and students alike. The advisors, who were with the guys at every moment, helped out when clarification was needed or the silence was too much. By lunch time, the students and MacLaren Youth Correctional Facility guys were excited to get out on the playground and have time together recreating. Lincoln boys and girls could hardly wait to roughhouse with the 'star' who had been in his/her classroom. Actually, some teachers got concerned that the roughhousing had gotten a little out of hand. I called Lonnie and the next thing I knew, the guys were organizing races and games and the playground had never been so calm. (That certainly helped the trust in this partnership from the teachers' perspective!)

Students wrote speeches that told how they had been influenced by the We 'R' One program and these young men who had chosen to chart a different course for themselves by helping others. More than one speech brought tears to the eyes of some 600 listeners attending the end-of-the year We 'R' One celebration. Christina still keeps in touch and cries to me about how difficult it is to choose the 'right' way and not the gang way when all of her relatives are involved in the gang lifestyle. Her friends are those kids who stay clear of the gangs. She attends church with her grandmother and has made a commitment to faith. She holds fast to the skills she heard and learned from the MacLaren Youth Correctional Facility men who joined forces with the educational arena in this community to help stop and prevent kids from that deadly gang lifestyle.

Nancy Merzenich, Counselor.

The response this program has received has exceeded our most optimistic projections. It has become a model of innovation and collaboration and has had a noticeable impact on resistance to gangs among the students in the school. The program received an education award from Woodburn Together, a community group, in recognition of what we have accomplished. The program has received positive media coverage and was featured at the National Governor's Conference in Washington, D.C. in 1995. Nancy

Merzenich was named the Oregon School Counselor Association's elementary school counselor of the year in large part for helping to develop the We 'R' One gang education and prevention program.

Self-Enhancement, Inc.

For the past three years, we have had a partnership with Self-Enhancement, Inc., an organization that receives national attention for working in schools and at its own center to provide education, recreation, and self-esteem building to young people in the community, particularly to people of color. We have been part of their summer youth project in which inner city youths gain exposure to things they have not had a chance to experience. These events include trips to the Oregon coast, Mt. Hood, businesses, and other places of interest.

As part of the partnership, Self-Enhancement brings groups from six middle schools to MacLaren Youth Correctional Facility for two weeks in the summer to hear our positive peer groups talk about what brought them to MacLaren Youth Correctional Facility and their plans for who they want to be when they get out. It has been an excellent experience for the young students because they hear from teenagers, who are close to their age, what the reality of gangs really is.

At the end of the summer, the Self-Enhancement children consistently vote the MacLaren Youth Correctional Facility field trip as one of the most rewarding parts of the summer program. The popularity of positive peer groups on campus is one of the criteria we use to gauge the effectiveness of our program. As the youths voluntarily participate in such groups, demonstrate leadership, and provide positive feedback to others, they show that they have internalized the principles we have discussed in our sessions. This form of validation enhances the effectiveness of our overall program. We also see how our participants are doing in other programs on campus. If they are doing well across the board, we know that they are achieving personal growth. Another criterion we look for is a desire to give back to the community when they get out.

beyond the walls: the critical need for aftercare programs

Background

We cannot be content with merely getting gang-involved youths to see the need to change. We also must be concerned with how they will work on that change and accomplish their goals to reclaim their lives. Much of their success will depend on how they handle situations that they will confront in the community. Will they get back into their old mode of thinking and quit when they face the inevitable bumps?

Regardless of the quality of any state correctional facility's gang-intervention program, it is unrealistic to believe that a gang-involved youth will experience a smooth and effortless assimilation back into the community. Numerous postrelease tests, challenges, and difficulties are inevitable, even for those who have developed a genuine internalized, personal commitment to redirect their lives.

Because of several issues, many youths will require a continuation of the services we provide for several months — and in some cases, years — after release. Today, more than ever, corrections staff members must have relationships with people in the community who will work with these young people once they leave the institution. We also must continue the work we began with them to assure their success.

The needs of each youth released from our program will vary greatly, depending upon a number of factors. Those who oversee the programs in corrections, the government, and our partners in the private sector, must work together to make a wide array of after-care services and resources available to meet the individual needs of each young person reentering the community. Youths, released from a program such as ours, may need community-based transitional services, including residential living, drug and alcohol counseling, support groups, job and vocational skills training, employment, mentoring, mental health, recreation, and opportunities to make positive contributions and enhance their community.

It is asking a great deal of the community-based programs to provide the support these youths will need until they are able to be self-sufficient and independent. It may be asking too much to expect them to start at square one with all youth and provide them with the impetus for a gang-free, crime-free lifestyle. That should be our job. We must help our community partners by ensuring that the youths we refer to their programs have seen the need to think and react differently to life's circumstances and have taken responsibility for their lives. With our assistance, the community-based program can help each youth build on the momentum developed in our program and continue to roll with it.

For these kinds of partnerships to work, we also must make sure that our philosophies and approaches are working together, so that there are no contradictions to confuse the youths. We must not unwittingly provide them with excuses to backslide and reoffend.

Minority Youth Concerns Action Program (MYCAP)

A vast majority of our African-American juvenile offenders come from North and Northeast Portland, Oregon. Most are returned to the same community when they are released. Many community residents knew that these young men would need help to keep on track and that without assistance, they were in danger of reverting to their old ways.

Because of this recognition of the need and out of concern for the future of the youth, a group of citizens came together in the late eighties, combined their talents and resources and founded Minority Youth Concerns Action Program (MYCAP) to help the young men paroled from our program to maintain their focus and achieve successful transitions back into the community. MYCAP's founders — Sam Pierce, Kathy Martin, Roger Wilder, Mary Omieff, Jimmy Johnson, and this author — had a good understanding of what we were doing at MacLaren Youth Correctional Facility and were impressed by the dramatic differences we were making in the attitudes of the young men in our program. We were convinced that the larger community would support a program to help our young men get on their feet. We also believed the young men could serve as role models to others their age who were gang-involved or at risk of becoming gang-involved.

Staffing the program was one of our main concerns because we knew first-hand the commitment necessary to work with these youth. Irving A. Spergel and Ron Chance of the School of Social Service Administration, University of Chicago have a criteria for staff selection that we thoroughly endorse:

> Gang project staffing calls for a thorough understanding of the complexity of gang culture and activity in the local community. A varied and multitalented staff should be selected that has a high level of ability, legitimacy, commitment, creativity, and the courage to overcome gang crises. Staff should be able to collaborate with a variety of other programs to overcome interagency political obstacles.
>
> [Staff should be] "well-trained professionals who are sensitive to the culture and identified with the interests of the local community and have experience in criminal justice, social service programming and/or neighborhood organizing; local influentials or community leaders who understand the interests, needs and problems of gang youth, yet who avoid using the gang structure as a mechanism for controlling or resolving gang problems; professional and neighborhood workers who together are able to establish socially meaningful relationships with gang youths — on an individual basis — and collaborate with parents, youth agencies, and law enforcement officers in the prevention, control and treatment of the gang problem (Spergel and Ron Chance, National Youth Gang Suppression and Intervention Project, 1991).

For nearly ten years, MYCAP has been a residential, transitional service program that has served youths from both the MacLaren Youth Correctional Facility and Hillcrest. A nonprofit organization, it operates independently of any Oregon Youth Authority program. Services include mentoring programs, employment, and employment assistance, treatment, and other support programs.

Although community residents initially were very concerned about having a residential program for known gang members in their neighborhood, they now are supportive of the program. The youths have worked on neighborhood revitalization projects, which have proven to the neighbors that these young men are an enhancement to their community.

The Success Academy

We have had partnerships with community-based organizations that establish personal relationships with our graduates before they leave the MacLaren Youth Correctional Facility. They help the young men devise personal goals and strategies for their success, and explain the value of more conventional dress, language, and interpersonal skills.

Due to our business partnerships with them, local clothing stores have provided new clothes (suit, white shirt, tie, and black dress shoes). Other providers have taken our young men to various settings to show them how they may be offered opportunities and advantages by presenting themselves in a way that is not threatening to mainstream society.

Cultural identity and self-esteem are important components of these partnerships. Individual strengths are emphasized rather than sacrificed for the sake of conformity. The essence of the programs is that to be financially successful, the youths must present themselves to others in a way that will inspire people to voluntarily invest in their success.

Some youths may balk at this traditional approach to dressing, but we explain this approach will help them market their skills and abilities. We point out that conformity has its purposes and that they already have conformed many times in their lives. We gently remind them that their urge to conform was instrumental in their decision to get involved in gangs in the first place. What we are asking now, we explain, is that they conform for their own good rather than for their demise.

Some of our partners and providers have given our youth a chance to make presentations at local Kiwanis clubs and educational conferences about the changes they have made in their lives This is a tremendous self-esteem builder.

The African American Male Transition Project (AAMTP)

The African American Male Transition Project is the most intensive, extensive aftercare program we have for our gang-affected youth. Funded by a federal Byrne Memorial Fund Grant and administered through Oregon's Criminal Justice Services Division, this project was created by the Oregon Youth Authority to address the overrepresentation of African-American males in juvenile facilities. As previously discussed, African-American males comprise less than 2 percent of Oregon's population, but in 1995, African-American males made up slightly more than 34 percent of Oregon's Multnomah County revocations, exceeding Caucasian males by 30 percent. This is not just an Oregon problem. The Sentencing Project, an organization critical of stiffer sentencing policies and the "war on drugs," found that nearly one-third of African-American males in their twenties were in jail, prison, or on probation or parole (Mauer and Helinge, Washington, D.C., 1995).

While we have ample evidence that our program in juvenile facilities does help break the mind-set that leads to criminal activity, we knew more was needed to help these young men find their way once they left our care and no longer had our daily support.

So, we created the African American Male Transition Project to study the effect of an intensive multisystem, culturally appropriate aftercare transition. We provide the services for five months after release from the MacLaren Youth Correctional Facility or Hillcrest, Oregon's second largest juvenile facility.

The project targeted African-American males returning to Multnomah County — specifically to North and Northeast Portland — which has the highest concentration of African-American gang activity. The primary objective of the project is to reduce recidivism and address the issue of overrepresentation of African-American males in the juvenile correctional system. Currently, the project has provided services for twenty-three African-American males in transition. The youths must be returning to either their family's home or to a foster care home.

The overall objective of the project is to reduce the high rate of parole revocations of African-American youth offenders by 50 percent. A 1994 study by Oregon's Children's Services Division found that African Americans have a revocation rate of 31.4 percent in the first month. A similar revocation rate was reported in 1996.

Recently, we added a Latino component to the project, and we are in the process of implementing a program for Hispanic youths in four Oregon counties. Youths meeting the basic criteria for participation are identified by our transition specialist, Damon Parsons. The youths are asked if they want to participate. Those who agree meet with the project manager, the support service person, and the minority affairs director at either the MacLaren Youth Correctional Facility or at Hillcrest, depending where they are serving time.

The support service person sets up a meeting with the Byrne grant team to develop a transition plan. He or she monitors the youth's progress in the treatment programs and arranges an educational assessment to develop an Individual Education Plan (IEP). After compiling all pertinent information, the Byrne grant team develops a transition plan based on the participant's individual needs.

During the youth's stay in close custody, he is involved with campus programs, including the minority services programs described in earlier chapters. The youth also may participate in groups for youths in transition back to the community. Our goal is to have the transition plan in place two months prior to the youth's release.

Within the first week of the youth's release, a transition team meeting is held in Northeast Portland. The youth, his providers, people providing specific treatment, a representative from minority services, the transition specialist, the youth's parole officer, and significant family members all are involved in the first meeting. As soon as he returns to the community, we show him that our plan is a reality. He knows our expectations and sees that everyone involved is on the same page.

This project requires tremendous cooperation between a number of organizations and individuals, including the Office of Minority Services, Oregon Youth Authority parole officers, a representative from the Department of Education, a representative from the Vocational Rehabilitation Division (if appropriate), community providers, private sector individuals and, when fitting, someone from adult corrections. One of the remarkable things about the African American Male Transition Project is the collaboration among so many people. This project demonstrates how concerned many people are about our youth and shows their willingness to work together to provide a solution.

Once the young men are released, they receive every service we believe they need to help them continue their commitment to turn their lives around. Our transitional specialist works with community service providers to ensure all their needs are met.

Presently, we have four community-based providers who offer services to our participants. Two providers offer mental health services, providing culturally appropriate counseling, conflict resolution, and anger-management skills training.

One of the unforeseen complications was the number of youth remanded to adult corrections who had been sent to the MacLaren Youth Correctional Facility for treatment. In many instances, if they completed treatment successfully, they would be paroled under adult correctional jurisdiction. We had many of these young men working hard in our minority programs who wanted to be involved in the project. We set up meetings with adult corrections and worked out an agreement that we would work directly with adult corrections so the youths could participate in our program. These participants got the best of both worlds. Not only did they get all the services provided under the African American Male Transition Project, but they also were eligible to receive all services available through adult corrections. Adult corrections assigned a parole officer specifically to work with the African American Male Transition Project. This kind of cooperation between state agencies involved in issues of criminal justice not only is inspiring to see, but it increases the chances that we, indeed, can help these young men turn their lives around.

Services

We provide a number of services. Each youth participates in all the services that meet his individual needs.

Education

We help enroll the participants in a high school that can meet their individual needs and arrange for individual tutoring, if needed. We literally have driven participants to school to ensure that they get there on time. When there are problems with attendance or performance, our transition specialist meets with the counselor and the youth to remedy the situation. Some of the young men return to regular public schools; others attend alternative schools because they cannot get back into a mainstream school. Some youths attend vocational schools.

Job Readiness and Training

Our service providers help our participants prepare for work. They help the youths prepare resumes, search for job leads, fill out applications, and prepare for an interview. We have set up an account to meet special needs and, when needed, we provide funds from this account for the providers to take the youths shopping for appropriate interview and work clothes. Many of our youths now are gainfully employed as a direct result of the efforts of the service providers.

Some of our young men are enrolled in apprenticeship programs. We contract with an organization that helps with assessing skills, developing job readiness skills, providing career development, and placing youth in work.

Preemployment skills include learning how to fill out job applications and work-related forms, writing resumes and cover letters, creating a list of references, learning telephone and interview skills, and learning the personal grooming skills necessary for interviews and the workplace. Job search skills include learning how to find job leads, using community networking, and cold calling. Work maturity sessions teach the youths good work habits, workplace behaviors, strategies for changing jobs, and the sessions provide information on workers' rights.

Mental Health Services

To address all the needs participants may have, we offer a variety of mental health services, including individual, group, and family counseling; anger management; grief counseling; post-traumatic stress counseling; violent offender counseling; and any other necessary service. We have been amazed at the amount of counseling some of our young men need. They have dealt with many serious issues in their lives, but without mental health services, many will not find the inner resources needed to carry through on their commitment to change their lives. We have young men who have known nothing but violence in their lives, young men who lost parents to drugs, AIDS, or violence, young men deserted by parents, and young men who have seen family members murdered. Not one of our participants has avoided serious trauma in his young life, and unless he is given the tools to deal with the aftermath of the dysfunction he has faced, he may have incredible difficulty overcoming past experiences.

It is often not enough to merely help the young man since the family he is living with is still struggling with many issues, so our mental health provider becomes directly involved with the family. Youths are sometimes resistant to seeing a counselor since they see it as a weakness, but treated gently, they see that it is a sign of strength, not weakness, to work through problems. We tell them, "Nobody could handle all of these things alone. You do not have to bear that weight." Resistance is eventually overcome and progress is made. Again, it may not be overnight, but the extent of the trauma is staggering, and there will be no "quick fixes" for the psychological problems the majority of these young men have.

Drug and Alcohol Counseling

Many of our youths have problems with drugs and alcohol. We make sure that they are in programs that address these issues. Drugs and alcohol are among the biggest temptations our young men face and potentially can undermine the progress the youths have made. It is critical that they stay away from drugs and alcohol.

Gang-intervention Counseling

We continue to work with youths on issues relating to gangs once they are released. We know it is very tempting to rejoin their old friends, and we must be completely behind their efforts to stay away from their old lifestyle. We hold regular meetings with all youth in which they support each other's efforts to forge a new path. More than once we have had situations in which a youth called our transition specialist for back-up help when there were threats from gangs. While we stress to all of our team members that personal safety comes first, our transitional specialist has intervened more than once when one of our participants was in danger. This proves to our youths that we are allies. It builds incredible rapport and confidence in our program.

Recreation

Along with all the hard work we expect of our participants, we also want them to see that life is good and that there are ways to enjoy it without turning to destructive activities. Our service providers take the kids to parks, play basketball with them, introduce them to sports they have not tried before, take them to movies, and out for lunch. They spend time with them talking and doing fun activities. The young men go the ocean and other places they never have been before. During these times, the service providers establish a firm bond, and the youth gains exposure to another way of living. One provider takes the youths to one of the area's most exclusive restaurants so that they can see that all of these places are within their reach; that they can be part of their reality. Some young men fear that they do not have the social skills to dine in fine restaurants, so our providers work with them to develop the skills they need and prove to them that they can be comfortable in any social setting.

Mentorship

Mentors are a critical part of our aftercare program. As mentioned in earlier chapters, many of our youths never have had positive role models and without a clear image of the right way to live, change is much more difficult. Many of our youths grew up in single-parent homes, and if they did have a father, it is likely that he was a negative, rather than a positive, role model. They often grew up with no moral foundation.

We turn to local businesses and churches for our mentors. The mentors from these sites are often people who work in the community at regular jobs who want to help their communities with gang issues. They have come from many different professions, including social services, and they may be state government employees, small business owners, and pastors. Our basic requirement is a genuine and sincere interest in helping a young man stay on track (See following box for mentor guidelines).

Guidelines for Mentors

When working with mentors, keep the following guidelines in mind:

1. It is best if mentors are aware of their own needs and expectations. Discuss this with them and be sure they are clear before finalizing any mentorship agreement.

2. Mentors need training and ongoing information to succeed in their volunteer positions. Promptly answer their questions. Be sure they know all resources that are available to them.

3. Mentors have the right to their own private life. Youths can demand a great deal from mentors; help them know how to draw the line. Their mentorship should be a positive experience for them as well as for the participant.

4. Mentors should be aware that the youths they work with may have different values than they do. While mentors are encouraged to help guide the youths, they may not impose their beliefs on those with whom they work.

5. Mentors should have their roles with the youths clearly defined. They are not expected to be therapists, social workers, or best friends. If the mentor feels the youth needs support he or she cannot provide, the mentor should let the mentor coordinator know so other services can be made available to the youth.

6. Mentors should set clear boundaries in their relationship. They should know their limits and ask for help from their coordinator if these boundaries are not being respected or if they feel they are being asked to go beyond their role as mentor.

7. Mentors must respect confidentiality policies and should not discuss their youth's lives and background with friends or family.

(continued on next page)

8. Mentors serve as role models to the youth with whom they work. Therefore, they should model the behavior they expect of their participant.

9. To ensure adequate time for the youth to relate to and believe in the mentors, the mentors should honor the time commitment they have agreed to unless they feel the youth's behavior is putting them in danger.

10. If the mentor has knowledge that his participant is doing something harmful or dangerous, the mentor should report it to the program coordinator immediately.

11. When the mentoring period is over, the mentor and participant should have a final meeting to say goodbye to each other.

We meet with the mentors and establish a relationship with them before they are linked up with the youth. We give them background information on the young man with whom they will be working. We are honest about the issues their youth has to deal with and talk about the strategies that will help the youth succeed. We try to match up mentors with youths who will be receptive to the mentor's approach to life. It is helpful if they have things in common, whether it is a favorite sports team, a common hobby or interest, or even the fact that they both were born in the same city or part of the country. These little things are often the things that help establish rapport. We make it clear to the mentors that we always are available for meetings and will answer all their questions honestly. Mentors have access to all of our support resources.

Each youth has a mentor. We let the youth and mentor determine how much time they will spend together. It is usually at least once a week. We also let them decide how they will spend their time together. Sometimes they go out to lunch, sometimes to a ball game. They may meet at a park. What matters is that the youth have regular contact with a person who will talk to them and show them that they do have options. Mentors help keep the youths focused and directed. They also become role models and, in our experience, some long-term friendships develop. More than one mentor has told us that being a mentor is one of the most rewarding experiences he ever has had.

Critical Success Factors

Part of what we provide cannot be categorized as educational, vocational, mental health, or recreational. It is difficult to define, yet it is one of the most important things we do for our participants. Situations arise that we could not have foreseen. There was nothing written in a book, manual, or program outline that has prepared us for some of the things that have happened; yet, it was critical that we acted quickly and wisely. How we have handled and continue to handle these situations ultimately will determine the success of our program.

For example, one of our young men, Albert, had a brother who killed a rival gang member. The brother of the young man who was killed, Ramon, vowed to kill Albert in retaliation. One evening our transition specialist, Damon, took Albert to a movie. When the movie got out, they were face to face with Ramon. Damon quickly got Albert out of the area and drove him home. Later that night, Damon received a call from Albert telling him that someone had just done a drive-by shooting at his house and fired several shots. Albert had every reason to believe it was Ramon. Damon wasted no time in driving over to Albert's house to make sure everything was all right and to ensure that Albert did not take matters into his own hands and go after Ramon for endangering Albert's family.

This kind of commitment and support proves to our young men that we are more than talk. We will be there. They can call us. Knowing this, more violence may have been averted that night. We contacted the Portland Gang Enforcement Police team to make them aware of the situation to ensure that they, too, would "keep their eye on things." Not only did we diffuse the situation, but we also averted violence that might have erupted down the road.

Another of our young men, Patrick, was released two weeks before his mother died. There were serious economic problems in his home, and he had two sisters who, at the time of his release, were dealing with issues of their own (one was pregnant; the other lacked necessary supervision and her behavior was out of control). One of our providers was with Patrick when he visited his mother in the hospital. He was with Patrick when she died. He attended the funeral with Patrick and made sure that Patrick got grief counseling. During Christmas, the family was in dire straits financially, and there was no food in the house. We found a community resource who gave them $100 worth of food. Despite the overwhelming problems Patrick has faced, he not only has stayed out of the correctional system, but he is holding a job and sticking with his commitment.

One of our young men was released to his aunt's care. She also was taking care of her niece. The niece had serious special needs, and the State of Oregon would not allow our young man to stay in the house unless both youth had their own rooms. Through our efforts, the basement was remodeled to make enough room for both of them. We also helped the young man's aunt get medical aid and provided other financial support for the young man in our program.

Our staff have done numerous other things for family members to ensure they have a safe, stable, productive life. One of the staff took a participant's girlfriend to a job interview. He often gave the participant's girlfriend a ride home from school to make sure there were no conflicts between our participant's need to get to work on time and his responsibility of caring for his child while she was not home. Our staff has intervened in school problems to make sure our youths do not drop out when there is trouble. They also have helped to resolve on-the-job problems.

Sometimes the participants make the wrong decisions, and we can see they are headed for trouble. We call a "time out" and put them in temporary custody at a juvenile facility so they can regain their focus. A parent once called us concerned that his son was not sticking to his commitment and that his son was acting the way he had before he committed the crime that led to his incarceration. We arranged for a "time out" for this young man and worked through the problems with him.

We cannot save every young man, but we can give them every opportunity to make good choices and the support they need to stick with them. One of our young men was murdered within a month of his release to the community. This was hard on all of us. We met as a group to share our feelings about his death and some of the participants received additional counseling. His death was a tragic reminder of the dangers our youths face and have to overcome.

Project Evaluation

No matter how good a program looks, no matter how strongly the developers know the program will have a positive impact, no matter how satisfied with a program the recipients report being, it is impossible to support the effectiveness of a program without sufficient evaluation. An evaluation provides a program manager with the data and statistical testing necessary to answer the question, "Did the individuals who received services provided through this program experience more positive outcomes than those individuals who did not receive the program's services?"

Under the best circumstances, an experimental outcome evaluation should be performed, including designing and implementing both the evaluation and the program simultaneously, randomly assigning individuals to the intervention (program recipients) and to the comparison (usual services) groups, and administering questionnaires and/or interviews to both groups before and after program services are received. Since this is very expensive in terms of both money and time, the alternative is to perform a quasi-experimental evaluation. The exact form of this will depend on the circumstances unique to the situation.

A quasi-experimental evaluation is being performed on the Minority Youth Services Program by Debra J. Elliott, Ph.D., Portland State University, Regional Research Institute for Human Services in Portland, Oregon, using a post-test with a comparison design. This method is being used because the program was implemented before the evaluation could commence; random assignment was not possible, and directly interviewing and/or administering questionnaires to both groups was not feasible due to funding and time constraints. The sample of youth used for the comparison group were matched with the intervention group for race, county of residence, and release to family or foster home.

These youth were selected from the Oregon Youth Authority's database of youth offenders, making sure that the youth were committed to a correctional facility (either MacLaren Youth Correctional Facility or Hillcrest) prior to the implementation of the African American Male Transition Project. The post-test used in this case was the monitoring of the youth in the African American Male Transition Project sample and the records of the youth in the comparison sample (in subsequent years, the comparison youth would be directly tracked) on the following outcomes: level of recidivism and status of either education or employment.

There are plans to alter the approach to securing and tracking a comparison in subsequent years of the evaluation by including a youth who enters the institution at the same time as the youth involved in the African American Male Transition Project. This would reduce the potential conflict of time (in other words, being released into the community at different points in time) and allow for comparable measurement of the outcomes (such as directly monitoring their progress) for both groups rather than relying on potentially incomplete records for the comparison group.

An interim evaluation was performed at the end of the first year of the African American Male Transition Project. Of the twenty-three youths who participated in the first year of the project, data on only twenty-one of them was used for the evaluation. One youth was excluded because his service needs exceeded the services available at that time (he was one of the first youths to participate in the project). The other youth was excluded because he was murdered approximately one month after being released. Nineteen African-American males meeting the postrelease requirements of the Byrne grant were identified by the process described and served as a comparison sample for this evaluation. Statistical analyses revealed that the two groups did not differ significantly on all of the following variables: average age at release, institutional placement, average duration in the institution, average severity of commitment offense, and commitment-offense category.

The level of recidivism (defined as returning to an institution based on a new or noncriminal referral) at three-months postrelease was lower for the African American Male Transition Project group (14 percent) than it was for the comparison group (32 percent). Stated in a more impressive fashion, 86 percent of the youth participating in the African American Male Transition Project did not recidivate! Also note, the recidivism rate for the comparison sample is nearly identical to the earlier-stated recidivism rate for the African-American males in Multnomah County (31.4 percent).

Looking at the recidivism offenses, it is notable that the crime severity dropped for both groups, with the greater drop for the African American Male Transition Project group.[1] A similarly positive finding was revealed for education at three months postrelease. The youths in the African American Male Transition Project group identified as requiring some form of educational placement were

---

[1] The sample sizes are too small to perform a significance test.

more likely to be enrolled in school than were the comparison youths,[2] with an inspiring 83 percent of the African American Male Transition Project youths actively attending school. Finally, at three months postrelease, 57 percent of those youths seeking employment were gainfully employed, in both the African American Male Transition Project and the comparison group.

Statistical evidence proves what we knew — our program has made a difference. Given support and services, our youths can reclaim their lives and become productive members of society.

---

[2] The difference between the two groups was not statistically significant (P=.10).

9

examining rap music

Rap music is a sensitive subject, so before getting further into this chapter, this author would like to clarify several points. This author believes in free speech, but he also believes that we need to acknowledge that music has a strong effect on kids. Whether you believe that heavy metal bands promote suicide or Satanism or rappers glorify violence and drugs, we need to take a stance against lyrics that encourage our children to engage in self-destructive or illegal behavior.

Acknowledging that some rap music may contribute to negative mind-sets and has the potential to increase violence among our youth is NOT to say that all violence comes from rap music nor that crimes were motivated solely by the influence of rap lyrics. Negative rap is just a piece of a far bigger issue.

This author is not advocating a ban on rap music, but we need to challenge our young people to consider how the music they listen to may contribute to their development and perception of themselves and the world in which they live. Rap music is certainly not the cause of gangs, but there is a relationship to gang activity that is an essential component of the gangbusters' program. Our concern is with rap music that promotes violence and negative attitudes toward women.

Increasing numbers of youths are flocking to recording studios to seek their fortune as rap artists. Using smooth and staccato lyrics, they declare their toughness and utter contempt for other rappers, and romanticize drug dealing, violence, and "gang-banging" in a form of rap music commonly referred to as "gangsta rap."

The music refers to young women as bitches and whores ("hos"). It glorifies committing homicide over something minor, such as a perceived "diss," a lack of respect or a put down. It constantly reinforces subconscious messages to our young men that there is nothing wrong with this way of living. In fact, it stresses that living a violent, criminal life is the best life kids can live; they do not need to try to grow beyond those walls because they cannot anyway.

One of this author's friends, a lawyer, has amassed quite a library of rap music. He listens to it, exercises to it, and studies it. He is a wordsmith who has long been fascinated by languages and cultures. He enjoys the humor, the tongue twisters and bravado, particularly of the more positive sort. He has memorized the lyrics of several of them. He could listen to fifty hours of the roughest gangsta rap without ever having a violent or criminal inclination. But the young men and women listening to this music do not have his life experience behind them, and so, unlike him, they are vulnerable to the messages of the music. Many young people are not mature enough to discriminate between the fact that some rap presents only one reality when there are many options open to each of us. Unfortunately, many kids identify with the situations of poverty, drugs, and violence in raps — and rap may contribute to their perception that they have no other options in life.

It is impossible to make sweeping indictments of an art form or particular artists. There are some artists who do a good job of describing the realities in our inner cities such as unemployment, racism, police brutality, the abundance of liquor stores, lack of economic growth, family deterioration, and black-on-black crime. Those topics are fair game as they are based on the real-life experiences of many people. Some rap artists deliver uplifting messages through their music, just as Negro spirituals have for almost two centuries. As a popular art form of our time, this music can be used effectively to instill self-esteem, direction, and motivation to pursue lofty goals. But that is usually the exception to the rule. Over and over, destructive rap music is used to exploit and hurt young African-American men and women.

For example, in an effort which was either misguided or insincere, a producer got several rap groups who identified themselves as either Crips or Bloods to come to his studio and record their most vile numbers insulting their rivals in a CD titled, "Crips and

Bloods Bangin' on Wax." The gangsters appear in their colors, flashing signs on the CD cover. One side of the album was called the Crip side; the other side called the Blood side. For almost an hour, the listener can hear the artists' rhythmic and rhyming lyrics about killing "punk-ass slobs" and raping "crab bitches." At the very end of the album, there is an excerpt of a postproduction discussion between the producer and the gangsters about the socially redeeming value of provoking, attacking, and killing each other with music and words and not with bullets. The conversation gave the impression that the CD was a noble exercise since the young men would be getting paid legitimate money for their time and efforts in the studio.

It never seemed to occur to the producers that other gangsters and "wanna-bes" would use many of its lyrics to psyche themselves up to validate the gangster lifestyles they were living. Perhaps they simply did not care that that was how the audience would use the music.

Most of the young men in our program listen to rap that is not uplifting, enhancing music, but the kind that confines their perception of their world within the walls of dope dealing, being a gangster, "gettin' your in's," having gold, money, and a fancy car. They pay homage to this mind-set by creating their own negative raps. The following is a rap piece we confiscated from one of our students who was still into that gang mind-set. It is transcribed verbatim:

B.G. PUT IT DOWN
Went outside
Jumped in my gee-ride
Went to the corner store and got a St. Ides.

I killed that shit on the way to the school grounds
I got to school and I'm feeling that s___
Now I was late but I did not give a f___
People was asking where my cousin L'il Click
I said I got to pick him up at 1 o'clock
Cause that nigga got my glock
Cause last night some punk ass nigga
Tried to serve on the block
So that nigga came out with the glock.

This goes on every day in P-town
When B.G. put it down
This goes on every day in P-town
When B.G. put it down.

Kickin it on the block
With my glock
With sixteen in the clip
Some nigga rolled by
And started to set trip on my click
I just was getting my slang on
But now I'm going to get my bang on
So later that day
I found out where them buster niggas stay
So I called my niggas up
So my nigga wicked got the fat ass strap.

In our sessions, we may study various artists and albums and note both the positive and negative messages and values woven throughout them. This is important because there are many nuances to this in-your-face art form. Understanding these nuances is crucial to help our youths understand rap as a description, not a prescription, of a world of which they do not need to be a part.

We examine what is really happening with destructive rap albums such as "Bangin' on Wax." We help the young men see how the talents of so many of today's youths are being exploited to create material, calculated to simultaneously entice and endanger so many in this generation. Eventually, many of them come to see such "art" as little more than hypnotic high-tech death warrants produced by some of its victims who, ironically, make lots of money for someone else.

Some try to defend gangsta rap, arguing that rappers, too, are describing the realities of their communities. We cannot deny that these realities exist, but we ask the youth whether these should be the only criteria artists use in deciding what messages to put into their minds?

There is nothing wrong with art describing the realities of the life of our times. However, the message should contain a ray of hope, not simply give the impression that there is nothing more to expect from life. The value of getting an education should be promoted more in our music. An educated African-American man with a strong mind is a very powerful force.

We do not want to knock rap music per se, but we do object to the way some of it is used. We have no problem with rappers speaking of issues in the neighborhood, but we do have a problem when rappers cross the line and glorify the violence that is destroying both our present and our future.

Until destructive rap loses its appeal, our challenge is to help the young men in our facilities see rap in the larger context. This is no small task because they are not yet blessed with critical thinking skills. In fact, few of them arrive at our facilities with any academic inclinations, whatsoever. They have had neither the desire nor the opportunity to examine their lives and their environments with the detached academic eye that the lawyer mentioned earlier has.

Music will be a daily part of our youth's lives when they leave our facilities. Because rap music is a popular part of today's culture, we do not try to isolate our young men from it, nor do we discourage them from writing and performing raps of their own. Rather, we present information about rap music in the larger context of societal and personal evolution. We help them consider the likely effect of being bombarded daily with catchy rhythms and rhymes and show how they become embedded in their conscious memory and subconscious mind, bringing about a gradual desensitization to normal, natural human concerns.

We admit that it takes a great deal of creative talent to write a good rap and mix it with a powerful rhythm and tune. But we ask our young men: "Why spend such energy and time creating a tool to get your people to terrorize each other and destroy themselves?"

Some of the more famous rap artists have tried to use their talents to turn youths away from the gang lifestyle and destruction that they and others have described and promoted in their earlier music. In one of largest collaborative efforts of this sort, about a dozen other well known gangsta rap performers put together a CD titled "We're All in the Same Gang." They open with a "We-Are-the-World" chain rap where each artist pleads with the listeners to stop committing acts of violence against others of their same race just because they are members of rival gangs. Throughout the album, they emphasize that the superficial lines gangs have drawn between themselves are ultimately meaningless.

But even in that CD, some of the artists maintained their tough-guy images, ostensibly to maintain credibility with those gangsters and "wanna-bes" who would hear the CD and view the video. Some might contend that their failure to entirely renounce the gangster and hustler lifestyles on the album was motivated by their concern for future sales of their other albums. One also might contend that such albums do not go far enough, because the ultimate message was not, "Get yourself together and live a productive, exemplary life," but rather, "Stay in your gangs if you want, but do not direct your violence toward each other."

We work hard to break down lyrics and to show how messages are reinforcing gangs, violence, and attitudes toward women that are harmful. We stress that all rap music is not negative and that there is nothing wrong with discussing problems and realities of our inner cities. What IS wrong, is the suggestions that drugs and violence will solve the problems or that it is not possible to have any other reality. Change is possible, change is imperative, and lyrics that create hopelessness can create the mind-set that leads to gang activities.

We celebrate when certain young men in our positive peer group write positive raps and perform them for group meetings and schoolwide assemblies. They use their raps as personal messages to those gangsters and "wanna-bes" on the outside who think they want to follow in their footsteps. We use rap to give options about life, to encourage supporting the family, to expose problems in our inner cities such as liquor stores on every corner, and a large school dropout rate. When kids write and perform raps, they have a chance to show their creativity and to create something positive for others.

The following is an example of a positive rap. It was written by two young men in 1994 who were sent to our facility for attempted murder.

P.O.S.I.T.I.V.E.
This rhyme is for the P, the P.O.S.I.T.I.V.E.,
I gotta lay the law about a Black history,
Back in the days life wasn't the same,
Our brothers and sisters walked around in chains.
I heard about the day that there was so much fuss,
When brothers had to sit in the back of the bus.
Well things have changed and got a whole lot better.
However, I say to myself I'm much clever,
We must fight and strive to be right,

Not by taking another man's life.
He likes to gang bang, he likes to sell caine,
What's going on genocide's the name.
Black on Black crime, eliminate gang signs,
Martin Luther King was a man with a strong mind.
He had a vision of us not to be violent,
I'm the G and I'm not keeping silent.

So wake up if you think that I'm tripping.
It is your life homeboy that keeps slipping, fight the power.

I'm on stage without a gauge.
I'm still in a cell, but I'm not a slave.
Dr. King died with a strong dream,
To stop the violence and kick the peace.

You see, when I was coming up
I was coming from the streets, banging,
slanging, hurting my namin'.
'Til I got popped, knew I had to stop,
Mom's getting mad cause I made her sad.
Almost took a man's life,
Over what, a drive-by?
Banging in the streets, naw, boy, you cannot survive.
This rhyme is for the P, the P.O.S.I.T.I.V.E.,
The P.O.S.I.T.I.V.E.
Stop the violence and kick the peace.

Section III

starting a new program

10

questions and answers for administrators: why give ourselves more headaches?

A friend engaged the author in a discussion of practical considerations associated with implementing a gang program at a correctional facility. Because many of the points he raised are cogent, the questions and answers are reproduced here. The discussion began with a hypothetical question that embodies both political and personal concerns.

1. *I'm the chief administrator at a statewide juvenile facility in our fifty-third state. We have had a staff of counselors and treatment specialists for issues of drug and alcohol, anger management, sex offenses, and mental health who have been together for fifteen years. They are very comfortable with each other. Based on statistics, things seem to be going pretty well. There have not been many instances of acting out within the walls. We have provided hours of documented service and the young men have been attending the sessions.*

Why would a person want to stray from the traditional tried and true ways of sex offender and alcohol and drug treatment for a program like the one you propose in your book? Why would I even want to invite political trouble into my institution, much less among the politicians, by implementing a gang program?

You have gang members in your institution. Can you demonstrate that your programs have redirected young men from gang involvement?

2. We hardly have had any fights in our institution. Youth attend the program sessions regularly.

That is not the issue. You have drug and alcohol staff to deal with people with serious drug and alcohol issues requiring specialized services. You have staff to deal with sex offenders. Yet, you are ignoring the growing number of young men in your institution who are gang involved.

Even if they are not presently acting out in your facility, unless you provide them with specific services that address the root behaviors and thought processes that led to their incarceration, you are doing nothing more than warehousing these young men until they are released into the community to resume their destructive lifestyles. This is an injustice to the community as well as to the young men you could have served.

3. I only can hold them for a few months. They go back into the community, and maybe they do reoffend, but when they come back, they do not cause any problems in here. What is wrong with that? As long as they continue to receive the instruction we give them, and as long as they behave themselves while they are here, what is our concern outside our walls?

One concern should be that you eventually will get greater and greater pressure from politicians and the community to do something if you continue to release guys who are gang involved, only to have them commit more violent crimes and come back again. People are going to wonder if you are doing anything more than just holding these guys here. Are you doing anything that redirects them? If you cannot come up with anything concrete, if you cannot even justify the types of interventions you are doing, you will have an angry community giving you a lot of heat.

Another concern ought to be the composition of your population. Presently, a lot of gang members are ethnic minorities. Do you have programs that deal with issues unique to racial minorities as wells as the gang culture? If you have more and more of that culture within the population, you at least should train your staff to recognize gang culture and dynamics. You can do what you consider is playing it safe, but you also ought to ask yourself if that is just.

You provide special services to sex offenders. You provide drug and alcohol treatment to those who need it. We have been creative in dealing with the needs of all other types of young people identified in the system. Should you not have specialized programs for the increasing number of gang members coming into the institution?

4. *Let me switch sides for a moment and add that there is a high school near my home. Odds are increasing that there is a gang or two about to form at the high school. I do not know who their coaches are, but the leaders must come from somewhere. It well may be that the gangs forming in my neighborhood are being organized by somebody who is incarcerated here. I have the opportunity to help young people make the decision to stay away from gangs. I ought to avail myself of that opportunity, because I ultimately maybe helping myself. That is why what happens on both sides of the wall matters.*

Right. Professionals who place too much value on the absence of serious incidents may be helping these guys institutionalize themselves. The absence of serious incidents, such as fights or escapes, may mean nothing more than the fact that the youths have learned the game of survival in the institution. These guys are not dumb. They have been part of the system. They know that the fastest way to come out is to mask the gangster self and do whatever the program wants them to do.

In this book, we described a young man from another state institution. He had reached the top level in his institution, and he had high privileges around the institution. But that institution did not have a gang program that included a dress code. He was allowed to wear his own clothes. There he was with his "Dickies," snake skin, blue belt, his pants sagging, projecting the image of a person still connected to the gang lifestyle. When asked what he was going to do when he got out of the institution, he replied, "I'm gonna bang," he said "cause nobody has showed me a reason not to!"

We have to recognize that we have a growing number of young men who think the same way. They require a comprehensive strategy of treatment and intervention. They have multiple issues to deal with, and like the sex offender or the addict or alcoholic who is in denial, they are hard-core resistant to reform, because being in a gang is their love. They are willing to die for their "sets." You cannot overcome their passionate devotion to their "sets" and the gang lifestyle with a minimal or token effort. The challenge requires a comprehensive approach that makes them check their thinking, their value system, and their actions.

5. *So, the purpose is to get to the root of the problem. You get down before square one and you start there.*

Right. You take a deep breath and look at what was there before there was a problem, and you figure out, square by square, how the problem progressed. I have had people in guided group interaction say, "Well, we do not deal with the gang, we treat it all as negative behavior."

But how can you get at the root of the problem if your treatment methodology denies the centerpiece of the kid's world? You put a "banger" in a drug and alcohol program and never touch on the issues of why he is fascinated with "gang-banging." These guys are smart, too. They can comply, but they do not really accept, or internalize the ideas to which they are exposed. They are sitting there thinking, "These guys do not know s— about me. They cannot understand why I'm gonna "blast" on somebody because they wear a different color." And, these kids are right. Adults do not understand how kids rationalize such actions.

A highly competent drug and alcohol treatment coordinator once came to this author for help with a particular student who was not only hard-core into "banging," but he was selling drugs. He kept making reference to St. Ides, and she couldn't figure out why or how Catholicism fit into the equation. She did not want to miss any opportunity to fully understand him. She learned that St. Ides is malt liquor beer popular in the gang culture. Armed with this information, she was able to help him further with his drug and alcohol treatment. Without a program that is specifically geared to gang-affected youths, and without staff willing to make use of the resources such a program can provide, important pieces of information may be missed.

The facilitator must understand from where these young men are coming. To be effective, the facilitators and staff of any gang-intervention programs must have an authentic insight into the experiences of the youths they serve.

6. *Something that you said a few minutes ago triggered a word that capsulizes the reason to have a gang-treatment program. It had to do with the fact that if you deal with every issue except the gang issue, the word "homesick" comes to my mind.*

You can control whether I speak or not. You can control where I walk. You can control what I eat. But you cannot control my thoughts. The only way to control what I think about is to have me work on what I think about. If I'm a gangster sitting through sex-offender treatment or music class and they do not apply to me, I'm still thinking about my "homies." I miss them. I'm homesick for my old life. At some point, I'm going to "be back with my own kind." Unless you give me reason not to want to go back to my "homies," as soon as I'm released, I'm going back to "kick it" with my friends. A person's internalized identity must be impacted.

This is his allegiance is to his "homeboys." He desires to rise in status in the lifestyle to which he is accustomed. He knows to get back to his homeboys, he first must get out. If he is around people who cannot help him develop his own good reasons to change and get himself going in a more positive direction, why should he change?

At the MacLaren Youth Correctional Facility, we wanted to demonstrate by our conduct that we are all the same. Former animosities based on colors and neighborhood must be rendered irrelevant because when you take away the colors and neighborhood identity, we are all African-American men. The thinking is the same in so many different ways. We did not want to have separate groups for rival gangs because we did not want to create or perpetuate divisions whose origins are based on the gang culture. We need to make the points with all groups in the same room.

7. *That brings up the issues: Why have rival gang members in the same sessions? What about the safety concerns? Wouldn't it be wiser to have separate groups for members or former members of each gang?*

There is a lot of fear about bringing former rivals together in an institution. Many would prefer to do nothing with them as long as they are not acting out within the institution. They prefer to use the traditional programs because they fear that bringing gang members together increases the risk that they will organize to plan assaults, attacks on staff, escapes, or strong-arm robberies of other students. They fear they might recruit within the population. These are understandable concerns, but with appropriate planning and preparation, they can be adequately and effectively addressed. There are several reasons for having people come together in the same sessions.

We have found it very effective to have people who, at one point, were willing to kill each other come to the same realization at the same time about the futility of such mind-sets and lifestyles. We want them both to experience it when we show them the suicidal mind-set.

Separate sessions for each gang would have the real and perceived effect of conferring status and power on each gang. It also would put them in a position of having time for their particular gangs. If rival gangs are not able to hear what we say to all gangs, we run the risk of being accused of discrimination or favoritism toward those identified with one gang or another.

We do have an Hispanic coordinator to staff sessions with Hispanic students in our facility, but that is primarily to address the cultural things on which we may not be as well versed. But there are former rivals sitting side by side, in those sessions, as well. We also have sessions in which youths of all ethnic backgrounds participate. We do not want Hispanics or others to develop "attitudes" toward African-American groups, claiming disparate treatment, services, and support. We also have Caucasian youths participate.

An overriding reality is that we live in a diverse society and to function effectively in this society, we must be prepared to interact with people of different backgrounds.

The Role of Self-control

8. *What can I do if I am one of only about a handful of African-American employees at a state facility where the African-American population is approaching 40 percent, half of whom are gang involved? I've listened to some antigang raps and heard some people talk about it. I even have heard some people say that white people celebrate when a black man kills another. How frankly should I talk about race and racism with the young men in our facility, realizing that all my supervisors and most of my coworkers are white? Are there some guidelines I should be aware of, or should I just take a chance of being unnecessarily provocative and irresponsible in my remarks with these young men?*

In our sessions, we talk about cultural pride and race relations. We want to impress upon these young men that there is nothing wrong with having pride in who you are and knowing your history. We feel you have to know where you came from to know and appreciate who you are and where you want to go with your life.

But as we work with these young men, we confront them with their own prejudices and bigotry. For a lot of these guys, the only people they can effectively communicate with are each other. In the gang culture, those who are not like them are "squares, busters, suckers," or something like that. They do have prejudice towards white people because they always have seen them as oppressors. So, what we are trying to do is help them grow as individuals, exposing them to their own culture and asking them if they are honoring their ancestors with the lifestyles they are living today.

Secondly, we want to help these young men see the true realities of gang activity, and to see that the consequences of this lifestyle are intolerable. Perhaps, they will end up victims of the system. They might get killed. Maybe they will do something crazy or just languish aimlessly. They might become an uneducated, unskilled, unemployed adult with no means of support, ending up addicted to alcohol or drugs, doing something crazy. They have to face those very real possibilities.

We have them take a look at their attitudes and expose them to cultural diversity. We have to challenge them and say that not every white person is a racist, and it is unfair to label an entire group of people on the basis of the action of a few or one person who has done something to you or because you grew up in an environment where the resentment of another group was standard. We have to respect the fact that there are differences in people. We show them that they do not have to love those who hate them or who are racist toward them, but they probably will work in a job in which they will be one of the few, instead of in the majority. They have to learn how to communicate to be able to prosper in such an environment. You can share this with your youth, and provide a model for doing so.

9. *So, what you stress is individual responsibility and the fact that they are responsible for their conduct. Whether there is somebody cheering when you shoot somebody or not, it is you who decide whether or not to shoot.*

There are many people who will "go off" when they hear the word "nigger," or when they learn that somebody is racist. If people know that you have a problem with racists, they are quick to jump on that — to exploit that fact and cause you to lose your composure and professionalism at the most inopportune time. This may close doors to your advancement into more responsible positions. So, we talk about racism in that context, stressing the fact that each of us has a responsibility to use self-control because there are always people out there who are willing to set you up and exploit your weaknesses.

We recognize that racism is still a part of this society; yet, our ancestors had to overcome a lot more than we do. Sure, there is much more progress to be made, but we are in a better position than our ancestors were, and our continued progress depends upon our growth as individuals. As we grow in education, stature, and skills, we will be in a better position to advocate and create. And along with skills comes self-control.

10. *Self-control is the part so many youths do not have. This is why they seek to identify with something greater than themselves, such as a gang, because they feel inadequate in themselves.*

Good point. After discussing gang realities and helping them see that they need to get serious and change, the next phase is to help them learn how to deal with anger and develop self-control for handling the various situations that cause them to fail when they would rather succeed.

A lot of guys have seen the need to change, but out there they are not strong enough to follow through when push comes to shove because it requires the ability to change and to know themselves well enough to handle difficult situations. Knowledge does you no good if you cannot apply it.

So, we try to give them tools they can apply when the peer pressure comes down on them. This is the point at which what we share with them is most valuable. They have got to start standing up for themselves and giving strong messages. That is why we work with them on handling their anger, using self-control, making good decisions, choosing appropriate friends, learning what a true friend is, developing self-esteem, and learning techniques of conflict resolution. This comes into play after we first give them the overview, the realities of their conduct and how it fits into a much larger picture.

11. *I see you and your staff as the coaching staff that has reviewed and studied game films. You have looked at the game from kickoff to final gun and studied each individual play of the game, and made note of the momentum and trends of the game, as well. After agreeing among yourselves what it is that you are seeing when you see it, you show the game film to the team. In your small group discussions, you will show them why a particular play worked or failed. You show them the series of incidents that led to the personal foul that cost fifteen yards. You literally show them how they got there and explain what they could have done to be more effective and in control.*

Exactly! This is a group of young people who have been highly volatile in the community. There is a thin line between success and failure. It is not just about getting them to see the need to change. Eventually, most of them will get to that point, one way or another. The greater concern is what it will take to get them to make that a reality for themselves. A lot of that depends on how they handle situations they will be confronted with in the community.

We tell them, "You're gonna have bumps here and there. Are you going to get back into the old mode of thinking and quit when the hard times come?" We stress the need for them to take individual responsibility.

You will have problems in the community. You will be confronted. People will even shoot at you because of your prior involvements. How you handle such situations will dictate how you turn out. We are not saying it is fair, but such scenarios may occur. Now, you have to have the commitment to redress situations in the appropriate ways. If you get shot at, instead of going to a 'homie' with the gangster mind-set, strapping on a gun and going after them, you go to somebody who identifies with your desire to ultimately be successful and you tell him what happened. He will probably tell you, 'No, man, you been doing good for six months, you're working. Yeah, it ain't cool, man, they blasted on you but going to get a gun, man, is just gonna land you right back in jail. And you have come too far.'

He's going to help you to stay out of trouble, make good decisions, and handle your frustration. And you eventually hope to pull yourself together and keep on striving. The message you are going to give all those other guys, even the ones who shot at you, is that maybe you're for real in terms of not being in the mix. They may still come, but maybe they'll think, 'Maybe he ain't bangin' for real no more.' And if you do shoot back at them, what's the end result? They're just gonna come back at you with even more because they will know you're still 'down.'

What about going to get your 'homeboys' to help you? Well, you've been telling them that you're for real about changing, but now that you got 'blasted on,' how are you going to get them to help you? When you go back to being positive, they're still gonna have beef out there in the community. When they have a problem, they're going to say, 'Hey man, this happened, we need you.' You cannot say, 'No, man, I'm back to tryin' to be positive.' You're going to have problems with them.' They'll say, 'No, man, when you got shot, you came and got us!' Now, you're gonna say, 'When we got problems, you ain't down? No!'

So the thing is, you have to make good decisions in this kind of a situation. Where one man will be dragged right back down into the mix, another will be ready for such situations, and use the tools we give him and make better decisions in difficult situations. He will live and grow as an individual. Plus, others will hear about it and support him even more when they recognize that he really is striving to turn around. The old him, they will say, would have been out there with a gun blasting back on them, being hurtful. Now he's trying to turn that corner.

In our program, we walk them through real life issues just like that. We are ready when they hit us with legitimate safety concerns they will have on the outside. We will say, "Let's frame this. What is the end result going to be? In the long run, who is going to be more successful?"

A lot of our messages are universal. Most kids hang out in groups of three to five people. They have negative friends and peer pressure. Many have family issues. The concepts we stress here have universal application. We are talking about alternatives that empower young people to be responsible, productive, successful people taking control of the direction of their lives.

11

blueprint for a successful gang-suppression program in detention and correctional institutions

Before you begin to set up a program like the one we have described, your institution needs to take firm steps to suppress gang activity. Suppression is the effort by the institution to stop conduct consistent with gang activity. Intervention, on the other hand, is an effort to interrupt a way of thinking or acting, to examine it from a fresh perspective.

Form a Committee

If you are about to start a gang-intervention program, start by forming a committee or task force to assess the unique characteristics of your facility. Develop policies, procedures, and criteria to identify gang members and to gather intelligence on gang activity at your facility.

This committee should lay the groundwork and decide on an appropriate structure. The committee members should honestly assess whether the present staff is sufficient for what needs to be done. They should decide if they should recruit or bring in a consultant.

The committee should strategize on ways to get the most staff support. You have to do it in a manner consistent with the atmosphere of your institution. Methodologies may vary from institution to institution, but there are certain features which should be universally involved.

Get Support from Administration and Staff

A program as intense as this requires the support of the administration and staff throughout the institution. It also requires constant reevaluation of methodologies to ensure effectiveness.

The administration must have a commitment to the program and be prepared to provide the leadership to overcome the resistance that naturally comes with changing the way services are delivered. Staff must have a strategy for rumor control and tools to defuse volatile situations, whether real or imagined. Staff must have reliable intelligence mechanisms to detect, defuse, and prevent explosive situations.

If gang graffiti appears anywhere in your institution, it should be treated as a serious policy violation. It should be photographed, documented, and immediately painted over to make it clear that graffiti will not be tolerated. A ready supply of paint, posters, and other devices should be on hand for a quick and effective response. If possible, the offenders should be identified and dealt with.

The facilitators need to establish ground rules concerning conduct and demeanor while in the group sessions, such as respecting the right of each person to be heard, whether you like him or what he has to say. The reality is that a lot of gang-affiliated young men realize that it is best to be neutral while in the institution, and have an agreement with other gang-members that, "If you have any 'banging' to do, let's wait 'til we get out." Hopefully, if your program is successful, by the time the youth get out, they will have given up "banging" all together.

Caucasian Staff and Minority Students

As we have addressed in earlier chapters, it is critical to have culturally specific programs staffed with members of the same ethnicity as the population you are serving. This is not to say that a Caucasian staff member cannot be effective working with ethnic youth. In fact, many Caucasian men and women have worked effectively with minority youth for years and know the population and the culture so well that they quickly gain the respect of ethnic youth.

However, it is important to realize that initially young men in gangs usually are going to be far more receptive to someone who looks like them and who comes from a similar background than they are to someone they have spent most of their life distrusting. Gang-involved minority youth are hard-core and, most of them see the white man as an oppressor. Part of the program is to help show the youths their own biases and prejudices, but this is best done in later stages of the program.

This does not mean the staff should be composed solely of individuals of the same ethnicity as the youth served, but staff members of the same ethnicity increases the likelihood that the youths will respond and be more open to treatment.

Cultural issues must be addressed. Treatment in juvenile facilities too often has been a "one size fits all" approach. Not only is this unfair to Caucasian youth who come from diverse backgrounds themselves, but it is almost certain to fall short in meeting the needs of ethnic youth.

For instance, violent-offender programs can be very effective, but gang members have killed for very different reasons than the typical violent offender, and if the reasons for their own violence is not addressed, their behavior is not likely to change. The same can be said of drug and alcohol treatment, sex-offender treatment, and virtually every other kind of treatment offered.

Many Caucasian people have dedicated their careers to working with troubled youths. They are intelligent, competent, professional men and women with advanced degrees. Many of them are fair in their treatment of ethnic youth and well may have marched in civil rights demonstrations and fully support equality on all issues they confront. To say that our ethnic youth may be better served by adults of their own ethnicity is in no way intended to minimize the excellent work done by nonethnic staff.

However, we must acknowledge that however well intended and culturally sensitive Caucasian staff are, when it comes down to it, youth of color may not readily accept a thing they say in the early stages of intervention. Many of our youths do not trust Caucasians. Real or imagined, they have grown up with the feeling that the white race is their oppressor. Why, then, would they listen to a Caucasian tell them they need to turn their lives around?

It is far more likely that they will respond to someone who shares a similar background. They probably will take the news that their lifestyle will get them killed from a member of their own community far more seriously than they will from someone they perceive as leading a life of privilege and ease.

They will be more comfortable in an environment of people like them than people unlike them. In time, if the treatment goes well, they will be able to recognize the value in what people unlike them have to offer, but initially, there will be strong resistance to a message of change given by someone they dislike and/or distrust.

Culturally Specific Programs

In an ideal world, we all would understand and respect each other, but we have not yet reached that goal. So, we need to take steps to ensure that our youths' needs are met while simultaneously bridging cultural gaps that divide us. This means that programs must be created that are culturally sensitive and culturally competent. When developing a program for minority youth, it is critical to create a culturally specific program and to develop a diversity plan. Unless you deal with the cultural factors that led to gang-activity and related problems, you will not effectively reach your target population.

As Marco Benavides, minority services coordinator for Oregon Youth Authority and a recognized expert in cultural competency and organizational systems change in Oregon explains:

> When some of the programs currently in place for juvenile offenders were created, they were created primarily by Anglo-Saxons to deal with a primarily Anglo-Saxon population. At the time of development, service providers analyzed the situations and asked themselves how they would meet the need for juvenile offenders. Many well-developed and effective programs were created, but at the time there wasn't a great deal of thought given to ethnic issues. Statistics show that in the past ten years, the ethnic population in juvenile facilities has more than doubled. Yet the same treatment plans are often in effect.

These are not effective because there was no considera-
tion for cultural issues when programs were planned and
implemented; thus, the needs of the ethnic population are
not being met. Staff needs the skills necessary to work
effectively across culture to meet the needs of the ethnically diverse population.

To provide more sensitive services, programs need to have two
critical components: culturally specific services and a culturally
competent organization. These two work together, supporting each
other, to create an effective program. Benavides explains:

When we say culturally specific services, we are refer-
ring to meeting needs of the minority population. People
from the same group who will use the services need to be
involved in the program. These people are usually more
aware of cultural issues and are often more willing to
incorporate cultural issues right away. Basically, this
means people running the program will be most effective if
they are from the same ethnic group as the youth they are
serving. They will be sensitive to issues youths deal with
in their everyday life.

A culturally competent organization is one that addresses cultural diversity in every aspect of the organization. Some key factors
include providing culturally specific services, diversifying the workforce, and creating an environment that welcomes ethnic minorities.

Another important issue to address is language. If youths do not
speak English as their first language, it is imperative to have staff
who can communicate in the language the youths speak and use
daily. This is not to say that all staff must be from the same ethnic background as the population they serve, but members of the
same ethnic group must be included and all staff must be aware of
cultural issues. Training programs should be available for all non-
minority staff to ensure they understand the many cultural issues
that must be addressed.

While it is necessary to have staff of the same ethnicity at the
early stages of the program, as the program moves forward, it will
benefit a youth to work with a culturally diverse staff that models
cooperating and understanding across ethnic lines. When dealing
with caring, supportive staff members of ethnicities different than
their own, the youth will begin to question assumptions they have

made about people based on race. They will see a larger picture, where all people can work together to create a better world.

Evaluating Your Program

To help you evaluate what steps you may need to take to initiate this program, we have designed a questionnaire to indicate your institution's strengths while revealing those areas that need improvement to successfully implement a gang-intervention program in your facility.

How would your institution answer the following questions?

The Institution

1. Does your institution have a clearly stated campuswide policy prohibiting specified gang behavior?

2. Does it have a plan for systematic training of staff on gang behavior, clothing, mentality, and graffiti?

3. Does it have an intake procedure which removes gang colors and provides state-issued clothing?

4. Does it have a commitment to confront gang behavior and impose consequences, when necessary?

5. Does it have a system for accurately identifying and classifying gang members?

6. Does it have a plan and adequate resources for the immediate removal of graffiti?

7. Does it have a well-reasoned plan and adequate resources to isolate certain gang members?

8. Does it have a well-reasoned plan and adequate resources to impose detention as a consequence for violation of its gang policy?

9. Does it have a well-developed plan and adequate resources to transfer certain gang members to other facilities?

10. Does it have a plan to systematically monitor the movement of gang members within its walls?

11. Does it have well-planned and adequately staffed support groups?

12. Does it have a well-developed plan and adequate resources to monitor improvements or deterioration of the behavior of gang members in its population?

The Staff

13. Does your staff understand and value the role of cultural awareness in reforming gang mentality?

14. Is your staff free to be flexible and innovative in tailoring strategies to the unique personalities among the population?

The Population

15. Are the youth in your facility continuing to identify themselves by their gang/"set?"

16. Are they planning, attempting, and/or executing assaults or escapes?

17. Are they recruiting and initiating members in here or from here?

18. Are they strong-arming others for cigarettes, clothing, or other favors?

12

finding support for your project

As we have discussed already, it may not be easy to get a program like ours off the ground. Some people will object to special treatment for minority students. Some will worry that it will upset the balance in the institution. Some will be concerned that bringing gang members together will cause more problems. We already have addressed these issues. What we have not addressed, however, is how to get financial support for a project like this. After all, staff has to be paid and community resources are not free.

General Support

Before you even begin to look for economic support, you must prepare and document your program. You need a written proposal with a mission statement, goals, objectives, and a well-documented explanation of why this program is needed. Articulate that you specifically want a program that addresses the unique needs of youths in gangs. Talk about the culturally specific issues that will be addressed. You clearly need to state what your program will accomplish, what you hope the outcomes will be, and what is needed to get the program going.

Be prepared to give an estimate of what the program will cost. Include salaries for staff and support services, as well as general costs such as for supplies, meeting spaces, and other operating expenses.

Include logistics of your program. Where will the program run? What will its duration be? What will the staffing patterns be?

Develop a curriculum that includes issues to be addressed and the structure in which information will be shared. Be sure to address safety and security issues for staff and youth.

Document all of this clearly, in writing. Do your homework. Review your documents. Make sure you clearly have shown the need for this program and your strategies to ensure success. Make as many copies as you will need. Hand copies out to all people who will be involved in the decisions to create the program and make sure you have copies for future funding sources. Do not rush through this process because it will be used again and again to evaluate the need for such a program and well may determine whether you get the support to create one.

Economic Support

There are many ways to find necessary economic support, including:

Grants

There are many sources for grants, from both the public and private sector. Federal, state, county, and city governments all have grant money available. Public libraries have shelves full of books listing organizations that offer grants. These books tell you exactly what kind of program each foundation supports. You may be pleasantly surprised how many people are willing to invest in minority youths. The federal government has funds for both prevention and intervention programs. At the state level, watch for Requests for Proposals (RFPs) that fit with your program.

Legislators

Lobby county and city commissioners as well as the mayor for support for your program. When you show them the value in what you are trying to do, they may become your strongest advocates. They are familiar with the issues in your community and often are helpful in finding seed money for innovative programs addressing youth-related problems.

Community leaders

Ask influential community leaders for support and to help you lobby to get the program off the ground. Even if they cannot personally make a donation, they may have some excellent suggestions for funding sources.

Private sector

Local businesses have a lot to gain by having safe communities and many have set aside a percentage of their profits for charity. It is to their benefit to invest in programs that will build strong community bonds.

Usually you will need to write a formal proposal to get grant money. Do not worry if you are not a grant writer. There are people available to help — sometimes for free. Newspapers regularly report on who received grant money. Take notes. Call these people and ask who wrote the grant. They will be happy to provide you with names and resources.

You must advocate for your program. Show how gang violence affects the entire community. Show how your program is designed to help stop the negative behaviors that are destroying our youths and our cities.

13

evaluating your program

You will need to have a formal method of evaluation to ensure ongoing funds for your project. Good sources include local colleges and universities and independent contractors. Because control groups are needed, this feature should be in place before you begin your program.

Do not be discouraged if the initial results are not as positive as you would wish. Use the results to pinpoint specific areas of weakness and then develop a plan that addresses those needs. Evaluations are invaluable research tools and never should be the source of discouragement.

If you want to develop an informal in-house evaluation to help you evaluate the project that you are planning, we suggest you ask these questions:

1. Does the program have a strong base in theory and research? In other words, how do you know the program will work?

2. Is the program age-appropriate?

3. Does the program address students from a variety of cultures?

4. Does the program include a strong focus on teaching social skills?

5. Does the program include a clear emphasis on changing specific behaviors?

6. Does the program allot adequate time on each topic to create behavior change?

7. Does the program include a clear emphasis on changing attitudes and norms?

8. Does the program include a strong peer component?

9. Does the program use a broad variety of media and teaching strategies?

10. Does the program include opportunities for its messages to be communicated beyond the classroom, for example, from the school, students' families, and religious and civic community organizations serving youths and families?

11. Does the program include training and support for the people facilitating it?

12. Does the program include an ongoing evaluation?

13. Do staff and students anticipate that the program will be both effective and enjoyable?

14

other minorities in gangs

In this book, we have focused on African-American gangs. However, many of the strategies outlined in this book have universal application, and, with proper sensitivity and planning, most, if not all, of these principles can be applied successfully to other ethnicities. Indeed, we do have an Hispanic coordinator, and we have Asian gangs in our population, as well.

There is one fact that all street gangs have in common, regardless of their ethnic composition: although they may be highly visible within particular communities, they actually do not represent the vast majority of the members of their communities.

Hispanic Gangs

The roots of several of today's Hispanic gangs can be traced to Southern California in the late 1930s. Immigrants fleeing the political instability of Mexico migrated into Los Angeles and Southern California in the early 1900s. Others came to the region from other southwestern states during the depression. Rivalries developed between groups of Hispanic immigrants according to the part of Mexico or the state from which they came.

The first gangs were formed in a climate in which each group claimed and defended its own turf, or portion of a geographical area, against invasion or mere penetration by members of a rival gang. According to Los Angeles Police Department gang specialist detective Joe Suarez, this aspect of the gang culture continues to this day. In his handout "Hispanic Gangs," Suarez tells us the following:

> *Hispanic gangs invariably name their gang after a geographical area or "turf," something they feel is worth fighting for and defending. Foremost in each gang member's mind is the belief that "the gang is more important than the individual member." This philosophy contributes to the perpetuation of gang activity by members, even with the knowledge they may die in the commission of such activity. . . . The relocation of a gang to a new area does not weaken their loyalty to the gang nor to the area in which they were originally formed. For example, three major Hispanic street gangs in the Southern California are named after streets that have not existed for years . . . . Hispanic gangs form alliances for purposes of strength. Intergang feuds and "wars" occur largely over territory or as a result of some real or imagined transgression by a rival gang.*

Asian Gangs

Asian gangs share very few of the characteristics of their African-American and Hispanic counterparts. Their dress is far more conventional. They blend into the general population and avoid detection. Secondly, they do not claim geographic turf. Rather, they consider members of their ethnic communities their turf. Asian gang graffiti is much more rare, as are tattoos. However, certain gangs, most notably the Japanese Yakusa, will maim themselves by cutting off the tips of their smallest fingers.

On the other hand, Asian gangs are very much like other gangs in that they tend to victimize their own people. Gang members occasionally commit drive-by shootings, usually against members of rival Asian gangs, but brutal home-invasion robberies by an entire gang "set" and repeated extortion of money from businesses owned by their own people are much more common.

In most instances, Asian street gangs are able to exploit the language barrier and the distrust of police which are cultural carry-overs from their homelands, especially among the Vietnamese. The likelihood of their crimes being reported is therefore quite minimal.

Gang-involved Females

Females get involved in gangs or with gang members for a lot of the same reasons young men and boys do. They face all the risks boys do, and then some. They face a high risk of being raped, incurring health problems, dealing with pregnancy and children, becoming welfare dependent, and participating in violent criminal activity.

This author believes that most professionals and volunteers would endorse the following concepts. First, staff should approach young women with the same level of commitment that they endorse for gang-affected males. Staff working with female gang members also should understand and appreciate the importance of modeling compassion, respect, and firmness without rigidity or anger. Programs serving females formerly involved in gangs should strive to develop the trust and confidence of their clients. To achieve this, the prudent staff will identify and remove as many impediments to such trust and confidence as possible.

For male staff, most certainly, self-control and good judgment are needed to avoid unnecessary sexual tension and crossing the line into exploitation of natural vulnerabilities. For instance, male staff participation in frank discussions of relationships and sexuality probably should be confined to defining and modeling "good" men and drawing distinctions between responsible, caring, long-term relationships, and those which are irresponsible and exploitative. Male staff, in conjunction with their female peers, should affirm the innate worth and human dignity of the young women in their programs and firmly insist that they neither use nor identify with terms such as "bitch," "skeeze," or "ho."

All staff dealing with young women should model healthy, caring, constructive, nonsexual relationships. Male staff must be particularly sensitive to group discussions about sexual behavior, particularly when the discussions include the sexual histories and sexual relationships of the young women. It is advisable to make sure a female staff member cofacilitates any such group or private discussions.

Finally, a program specifically tailored to young females should include discussions of health issues, child rearing, and breaking the vicious cycle of poverty and welfare. The program should be very strong in building self-esteem and instilling a sense of self-worth in the participants. Such programs always should affirm a woman's right to protect her children and herself by avoiding or renouncing all unhealthy relationships, which pose a threat to their health and liberty.

references

American Correctional Association. 1994. *Gang Management Strategies in Corrections, Video*. Lanham, Maryland: American Correctional Association.

———. 1997. *Gangs: The Fatal Attraction Video*. Available from American Correctional Association, Lanham, Maryland.

———. 1998. *Supervising Young Offenders Video*. Lanham, Maryland: American Correctional Association.

Bownes D., and S. Ingersoll. 1997. *Juvenile Justice Bulletin*. July. Washington, D.C.: Office of Juvenile Justice and Delinquency Prevention.

Glick, B., W. Sturgeon, and C.R. Venator-Santiago. 1998. *No Time to Play: Youthful Offenders in Adult Correctional Systems*. Lanham, Maryland: American Correctional Association.

Glick, B. and A. Goldstein. 1995. *Managing Delinquency Programs That Work*. Lanham, Maryland: American Correctional Association.

Mauer, M. and T. Helinge. 1995. *Young Black Americans and the Criminal Justice System: Five Years Later*. Washington, D.C.: The Sentencing Project.

references

Morton, J. Ed. *Complex Challenges, Collaborative Solutions: Programming for Adult and Juvenile Female Offenders.* Lanham, Maryland: American Correctional Association.

Office of Juvenile Justice and Deliquency Prevention. 1995. *National Youth Gang Survey.* Washington, D.C.

Spergel, I. A., and R. Chance. 1991. *National Youth Gang Suppression and Intervention Project.* Chicago, Illinois: University of Chicago.

appendices

appendix A

Oregon Youth Authority

The programs described in this book are all part of the Oregon Youth Authority (OYA). Oregon Youth Authority's mission is to protect the public by holding youth offenders accountable and by providing opportunities for reformation.

Established on January 1, 1996, the Oregon Youth Authority assumed responsibilities for services to youth offenders previously provided by Oregon's Children's Services Division of the Department of Human Resources. Oregon Youth Authority provides a continuum of services to protect the public and reduce juvenile crime through Oregon Youth Authority programs and partnerships with local communities and counties. The Oregon Youth Authority emphasizes decisive intervention in delinquent behavior, certain sanctions for crimes committed by youth, restitution to victims, and effective and innovative rehabilitation for youth offenders.

The Office of Minority Services is a branch of the Oregon Youth Authority. Its mission is to provide and support culturally specific and language-appropriate programs and services to address the complex issues faced by the culturally and ethnically diverse youth in the Oregon Youth Authority system.

The Oregon Youth Authority and Office of Minority Services staff have developed a wide range of programs and services, including positive peer groups, special events, partnership programs such as the African-American/Latino Male Transition Project, the Gang

Tattoo Removal Program, the Minority Youth Concerns Program, ethnic advisory committees, and other programs.

Partnerships are essential in dealing with the issues ethnic youth face. Minority Services has developed partnerships with the following organizations:

- African-American Legislative Leadership Roundtable

- Department of Education

- Diversity in the 90s Steering Committee

- Governor's Juvenile Justice Crime Prevention Taskforce

- Hispanic Services Roundtable

- Northeast Rescue Plan Action Committee

- Oregon Psychiatric Association Steering Committee on Gangs

- Over-representation of Minorities/System Change Committee

- Salem/Keizer Gang Project

- State Commission on Black, Hispanic, Native American, and Asian Affairs

- Vocational Rehabilitation Department

As someone who is employed by Oregon Youth Authority, this author has been extremely impressed with the vision and understanding needed for the balance of public safety issues, accountability of the juvenile offenders, and the reformation/rehabilitation of the juvenile offender. The agency's willingness to develop partnerships and take risks to accomplish these objectives is impressive. The staff has worked unselfishly and shows consistent commitment to making a difference in the lives of Oregon's youth.

While only slightly more than two years old, the Oregon Youth Authority's innovative programs and approaches to administering juvenile corrections is a model for other states.

appendix B

Testimonials: Editorial on We R One

The following editorial appeared in the Woodburn Independent on June 21, 1995:

More than 500 parents turned out last Tuesday for a barbecue to salute an innovative new program at Lincoln Elementary that enlists ex-gang members to teach children that crime doesn't pay.

The pilot program, called We 'R' One, is the brainchild of Lincoln counselor Nancy Merzenich and MacLaren minority affairs coordinator Lonnie Jackson. Every other week four young men — incarcerated for crimes ranging from burglary to murder — spend a day with Lincoln students, sharing their own hard-learned messages about friendship, respect and responsibility.

Lincoln, more than any other Woodburn elementary school, is plagued by gangs. Many of its students come from gang families or count gang members among their friends. So, last fall, Merzenich and Jackson proposed We 'R' One to a skeptical community.

Many parents balked at the program, believing that young criminals would only encourage their children to follow in their footsteps on the road to ruin. A meeting organized by Merzenich and Jackson to explain the program to parents drew only three people.

However, We 'R' One has proved its critics wrong. The program has united Lincoln students, who proudly wear their We 'R' One T-shirts to school. And it has opened their eyes to the consequences of gang affiliation.

MacLaren youth are frank in their assessment of gang life, warning children to steer clear of the easy money, crime and drugs that lured them into joining gangs and eventually landed them in the corrections facility. They miss their friends, their family and their freedom. They do not want to see other children make the same mistakes.

This unique partnership has attracted plenty of attention from educators across the country. A Los Angeles film crew recently visited Lincoln to create a videotape documenting the program's success; the resulting program was featured during the National Governors' Association convention on Tuesday, June 6.

Educators should consider We 'R' One to include all Woodburn schools. The program packs a powerful message for youth, a message made more meaningful by a handful of young men who have owned up to their mistakes and shown their willingness to repay society by befriending Woodburn's children.

Letter of Support from Rick Hill

Rick Hill is the director of the Oregon Youth Authority. He also served as superintendent of MacLaren during the early years of the Minority Youth Concerns Program.

As the director of the Oregon Youth Authority and the former superintendent of MacLaren Youth Correctional Facility, I want to tell you how important Lonnie Jackson's Minority Youth Concerns Program has been to me and to this agency.

With gang violence erupting in this country's correctional institutions, it may seem counterintuitive to endorse a program that brings rival gang members of different ethnic and cultural backgrounds together in one room for treatment sessions, but that is exactly what Mr. Jackson's program does on a regular basis at MacLaren Youth Correctional Facility. Trusting Lonnie's instincts and setting my own fears aside was the best decision I made as superintendent of MacLaren. For nine years running, MacLaren — an institution of over 400 youth offenders — has been virtually free of racial and gang-related incidents.

The impact of Minority Youth Concerns has gone beyond the absence of violence. It has brought staff and youth alike together in a new and ongoing appreciation for cultural diversity. We have all learned the importance of working together and the value of learning from each other. By providing multi-racial, multi-cultural events such as our Black History Assembly and Cinco de Mayo celebrations, we have opened our institution to outside community organizations that enrich our program.

I believe that the Minority Youth Concerns Program described in *Gangbusters* can easily be recreated in other juvenile institutions. It is well worth the administrative support and will pay off almost immediately with a reduction of violence within the facilities, and have a longer term aftercare impact as well. I strongly encourage other institutions and agency administrators to read *Gangbusters*.

Sincerely,

Rick Hill

appendix C

Glossary

A	Ace Cool/Ace Kool	best friend/partner/back-up
B	Bank	lots of money
	Base head	cocaine smoker
	Beatdowns	physical assaults
	BKA	Blood killer always
	Bo	marijuana
	Book	run, get away, leave, take off
	Boned out	quit, chicken out, turn tail
	Bow	marijuana
	Break	run, get away
	Breakdown	shotgun
	Bucket	older beat-up car
	Bullet/bullet	one-year sentence
	Bumping titties	fighting
	Bustin a nut	having sex with a female
	Busted	arrested or shoot at someone
	Buster	person who wants to be a gangster
	Busting	involved in a fight with fist or weapons

C	Check in out	listen to what I have to say
	Chill out	take it easy, stop it, do not do it
	Clocking dollars	making money
	Cluck	cocaine smoker
	Colum	Columbian marijuana
	Crab/krab	derogatory term for Crip gang member
	Chagared down	low-rider carefully dressed gang-banger
	Crumbs	tiny pieces of rock cocaine
	Cuaa	Crip gang member
	Cuzzin	Cripping gangstering
D	D	drugs
	Deuce and a quarter	Buick Electra 225 car
	Dime speed	10-speed bike
	Do a ghost	to leave the area
	Doing dirt	doing negative, criminal activity
	Double deuce	22 caliber gun
	Down for mine	ability to protect self
	Drop a dime	squeal on someone, to snitch
	Durag	handkerchief used as a head wrap
	Drive-by	shooting from a moving vehicle
	Dusted	under the influence of PCP
E	Ends	money
	Essay	friend
F	Firing on someone	throwing a punch or shooting at someone
	Four-five	45 caliber handgun
	Freak	pretty girl
	Fresh	latest style or trend
G	Gage	shotgun
	Gat	gun
	G-ride	gangster ride, stolen vehicle
	Gang-banging	person involved in gang activiety
	Get with him/her	either fight or meet someone

	Get down	fight/to be serious
	Getting waxed	having sex with a female
	Glass house	'77-'78 Chevy
	Gig	gathering, a social function
	Got it good	had lots of drugs
	Got it going on	well-off, engaged in illegal activity
H	Hard	tough
	Ho	whore
	Holdin down	controlled turf or area
	Homeboys	friends
	Hood	neighborhood
	Hook	phony, imitation, punk
	Hoopty	car
	Hoo rah	loud talking
	Hubba	rock cocaine
	Hustler	individual "street" money maker
I	In the mix	busy, involved in gang activity
J	Jack move	robbery, criminal activity
	Jacked up	confronted, pressured; vehicle rear, riding high
	Jammed	confronted, placed in awkward position
	Jiving	attemping to fool someone, lying
K	Kibbles and bits	tiny pieces of crack cocaine
	Kicking back/kicking it	taking it easy
	Knocking the boots	having sex with a female
L	Lady	girlfriend
	Let's bait	let's leave
	Lifts	vehicle hydraulics (Up/down)
	Lit up	shot
	Live large	living fancy, materialistic lifestyle
	Loc	loco/Crip

	Lok	loco/Blood
	Love	rock cocaine
M	Mackin	individual solely interested in girls
	Main man	best friend, back up
	Making bank	making money
	Man	law officials
	Mark	want to be a gang member
	Molded/scratch	embarrassed
	Monte C	Monte Carlo vehicle
	Mission	contract hit, taking care of business
	Mud duck	ugly girl
N	N-H	neighborhood
O	O/G	original gangster
	On the pipe	free-basing cocaine
	One time	police in the area
P	Packing	gang member carrying handgun
	Playboy	ladies' man
	Player	individual solely interested in girls
	Pugging	fighting
	Put 'em in check	discipline someone
	Put in some work	do a shooting
	Puffer	cocaine smoker
R	Rag	color of gang handkerchief
	Raise	leave
	Rasberry	female takes anything for sex/drugs
	Rock	crack cocaine
S	Skeezers	whore; woman who does drugs and leads a sleazy lifestyle
	Slangin	selling drugs
	Soft	weak

	Step to me	challenge
	Sucker crews	Rival gangs
W	Wanne-bes	Someone who wants to be a gang member

about the author

Lonnie Jackson grew up in a gang-infested area of South Central Los Angeles, so he has first-hand experience of the lives of youth in gangs. Then, he attended Willamette University in Salem, Oregon where he earned his B.S. degree in sociology and psychology. After he completed college, he began working at the MacLaren Youth Correctional Facility, where he developed the gangbusters program described in this book. In 1993, he received a grant from the U.S. Information Agency to conduct a community action and drug prevention project in Bangkok, Thailand.

Mr. Jackson is now the statewide director of Minority Services for the Oregon Youth Authority. He believes that "if you give youth a realistic approach to life and replace helplessness with hopefulness, there will be more successful youth than failed youth." His programs offer visible proof of this contention.

This book and his lectures help individuals to understand the mind-set of gang members, the factors that are involved in the formation of gangs, the rationale for programs to rehabilitate gang youth in institutions and correctional facilities, and to develop suppression strategies for gang youth in correctional facilities and innovative intervention strategies designed to break through the hard-core mind set of gang members.

Lonnie Jackson has received numerous awards and citations for his achievements, including the first KGW-TV Citizenship Award, the Ruby Isom Award for Outstanding Accomplishments in Juvenile Corrections, and the Model of Excellence Award from the Delta Kappa, Inc. national sorority. He also has received the Willamette University Distinguished Alumni Award, and the Compton Award from the Marion County Bar Association for extraordinary service to the bar and the judicial system.